ROCKING
YOUR ROLE

The 'how to' guide to success for female breadwinners

Jenny Garrett

Rocking Your Role

First published in 2012 by: Ecademy Press

48 St Vincent Drive, St Albans, Herts, AL1 5SJ

info@ecademy-press.com

www.ecademy-press.com

Printed and bound by Lightning Source in the UK and USA

Design and Typesetting by Charlotte Mouncey

Printed on acid-free paper from managed forests. This book is printed on demand, so no copies will be remaindered or pulped.

ISBN 978-1-908746-20-7

Praise for Rocking Your Role

"A rare and powerful book covering an immensely important subject in a personal, practical and very moving way. I was inspired by reading it and left breathless by the achievements of the author and the women whose stories she tells."

DR ANN LIMB OBE DL, CHAIR, SOUTH EAST MIDLANDS
LOCAL ENTERPRISE PARTNERSHIP

"Reading this book lifted the clouds of expectations, guilt, imaginary limitations.... it liberated me to pursue my own personal dreams while still providing for my family."

NADINE JUIGNET, BUSINESS DEVELOPMENT
ADVISOR AT HEWLETT PACKARD

"This is a well researched book, that I think will meet a real need, the practical exercises are welcomed, much better than just a pile of theory. Perfect for those women struggling with being breadwinner."

HEATHER MCGREGOR, AUTHOR,
CAREERS ADVICE FOR AMBITIOUS WOMEN

"Jenny's insightful work is clearly founded on a deep understanding of the dynamics of relationships and careers, and on the ways in which people develop and learn, as well as on her interviews with women specifically for this book. I wish Rocking Your Role well; a book like this, should it become a top seller, will do more to transform the lives of women, and those of their partners and families, than any number of Government commissions."

PHILIP WHITELEY, BUSINESS AUTHOR

"Jenny has a great writing voice and has bought a human touch to a taboo subject with great sensitivity and creativity."

JACKEE HOLDER, COACH, AUTHOR,

"Jenny Garrett charts the rise of the female main earner (ME) in her highly engaging exploration of female breadwinners. That a fifth of women in the UK now earn more than their partners is significant, yet we hear little about this. This book is an invaluable and inspiring source for those who will, either through choice or by chance, embark on this exciting route. She offers advice and space to reflect and challenges one of the modern day taboos."

MARY HONEYBALL MEP, LONDON MEP AND
LABOUR EUROPEAN SPOKESPERSON ON WOMEN

"From the moment I started reading Rocking Your Role I was totally absorbed, recognising so many of the issues that Jenny refers to within this clearly written and practical book. She takes the reader on a journey which makes you question yourself in a way that energises you to step back and think about your work life balance, and the importance of being honest with yourself and those around you. It will resonate with successful women, especially those who are the female breadwinners, in all areas of life."

PIM BAXTER DEPUTY DIRECTOR,
NATIONAL PORTRAIT GALLERY

"Jenny is an inspirational role model and her book provides a practical guide to huge possibilities if we heed her liberating advice. I felt hugely empowered as I worked through the exercises and loved her "ego check" section. A must read book for every woman which I will buy for my dearest girl friends."

LYNNE SEDGMORE CBE, EXECUTIVE DIRECTOR
OF THE 157 GROUP OF FE COLLEGES

For Sunshine and Bear.

Acknowledgements

Thank you to all the women who I interviewed as part of this research. You are an inspiration; my modern day heroines who have made this book possible.

Immense gratitude to Rose who nurtured the seed and Mindy who helped me make it a reality.

I am so grateful to my husband Rob, daughter Leah and many friends and family for your encouragement.

Lastly, a special thank you to my mum Mary, who has always believed in me.

Contents

Introduction

I feel that I need to start this book by introducing myself as I might do at an AA meeting. Hi, my name is Jenny Garrett and I am the main earner (or ME as I will refer to it in this book) for my family. It's not because being ME is an addiction, but because it is perhaps one of the last taboo subjects in society and, as such, something that you don't usually declare publicly.

There are, of course, a growing number of single parent families where often, but not always, the mother brings up the children. There are also an increasing number of women who don't have children and are solely responsible for their households. Both of these circumstances have their difficulties and opportunities.

However, the situation which is least spoken about is when a couple is co-habiting or married, with children and the woman is the main or sole income earner. *Shhhh, don't tell anyone, it is one of the last taboos* and the one that we will focus on together.

It is difficult to find career women who have young children and are married or co-habiting. They might disclose two of the three things to you, but not all three.

You may wonder why it matters. Well, I think it's because anything that is unsaid and kept in the shadows doesn't get the light of examination and scrutiny placed upon it and, as such, doesn't get supported, challenged, celebrated or denigrated. Instead assumptions will be made, statements left unchallenged and life goes on; or does it? My experience is that you will be dealing with the internal and external issues of being ME in isolation and unsupported.

Through this book, I aim to supportively challenge you, help you generate ideas and be inspired to make your experience of being ME work for you.

My story

I am sharing a bit about me, so you can understand my history and perspective when writing this book. This is what forms my experience of being ME and no doubt your history will inform yours. I was born in 1971 to a teenage mother in north west London. Both my parents emigrated to the UK from the Caribbean at an early age. Some, or should I say most, would have predicted that the future didn't look bright for me. My father was not absent, but didn't live in the same house from when I was about 2 years old, though he was always available to me and visited on a regular basis. However, I wasn't missing male role models; my mother has three brothers, and my grandfather was always around.

At the age of 8, the best brother I could have wished for came along and my stepfather had arrived some time before that. I lived in council accommodation, starting off in an estate with flats twenty stories or so high; if it was the US, you would call it the projects. I have distant memories of the smelly lift and the rubbish chute, which always intrigued me.

I am not sure at which point in my childhood I became acutely aware that it was me and Mum against the world, but I think I was still in single digits. I know from that point onwards I was fiercely independent, not wanting to burden my Mum with asking for things and definitely not demanding anything that cost money because I knew it was tough for us.

From the age of fourteen, I worked in a newsagents on a Sunday morning to try to buy the things I wanted. I held the ethos that I would need to work very hard to get anything and even then there might never be enough. This was not seen by me as negative. I didn't feel like a victim at the time nor have I done so since. It was just the way it was.

In the late 1990s, I became interested in leadership coaching, thanks to a strong, inspiring and determined female colleague and friend, also a ME. Training as a coach was the catalyst for a transformational change in my life, helping me to be more self-aware, confident and live life to the full.

This change created space for me to encourage my husband, who had been unhappy at work, to seek opportunities more aligned with his values. He did this successfully and became a college lecturer, during which time my work took off as a leadership coach and facilitator and I completed a part-time Masters degree.

This shift and change is at the heart of me as ME. The balance shifted; my husband was happier in his role, although his salary was lower than he had earned previously while my work took off, making me happier as well but now in the new role as ME. So why bother to analyse the experience? Because there were many internal and external challenges that I had to overcome - my own thoughts and feelings about my role as ME in the family - dealing with others' perceptions and finding ways to make it work for everyone - that you may be facing too.

I have learnt some lessons along the way and hope that my experience and that of the other women MEs in this book will help you avoid them, or at least become more aware in order to make the very best of your current situation.

I don't apologise for this book being from a woman's perspective; I believe this is the voice that is least heard. But this is not only a book for women, as it can also help men to understand the female experience of being ME.

Rising MEs

Increasingly in my work coaching leaders in the UK and US and facilitating leadership programmes, I come across women leaders who are MEs in their family. You may be ME because your partner has been made redundant, laid off, retired, is unwell, or perhaps it is down to circumstance and choice.

Figures from a government commissioned report into economic inequality, published by the National Equality Panel in 2010 show that one in five women in the UK are the breadwinner, earning more than their spouse or partner. This equates to around 2.7 million women and the number is likely to have grown since then. The growth of female breadwinners is not unique to the UK, it is higher in the US, which Reuters reported to be one in three in the same year. A recent Twitter response to my question, 'What has been the most significant change for you over the last 12 months?' was: 'Only one of us is employed and we have had a significant decrease in our overall income and now it's all down to me!' Often juggling work, life and family in secrecy, this growing number of MEs rarely discuss or seek coping strategies for their complex role in the world.

This dynamic is new to Western society, but not new to the world as a whole. Women were, and still are in some African tribes, accepted hunter gatherers. They go out and hunt the dinner while the men tend to the chores at home. I have used a thimbleful of their wisdom in this book and have interspersed African proverbs to inspire and guide you.

So what?

The shift to ME can fundamentally challenge your identity and the assumptions made by those around you. For a successful career and family life you must examine and address these challenges.

Being ME is not the issue on its own, but it is the trigger, catalyst, and cause for many complex internal issues that you have to manage. These must be addressed for your physical, mental, and spiritual wellbeing.

I value an understanding of the social and political factors that impact women's lives, and have read widely around the subject of female breadwinners, but often find the literature lacking when it comes to translating it into action. There are some interesting references at the back of this book so that, if you wish, you can engage in further reading and research on the subject.

However, this book is concerned with *you* designing *your* best life in *your* current and unique situation. It is not just designed to be informative; rather it is designed to be transformational, so it's intensely personal and practical.

Guidance

This book is created as a guide for you in your life as ME. It is carefully designed to supportively challenge you through the internal and external issues and opportunities you face, in order to make the most of your role and make your corner of the world work for you.

Each chapter is focused on an area that you will need to work on as ME. Based on the experiences of women MEs, the book was written as a sequential developmental process to engage in. To make the most from the book, you should take a chapter a week and engage in the twelve week process. At the end of that time you can chart your progress and plan how to sustain it. However, I know whichever way you engage with the book will be the best way for you.

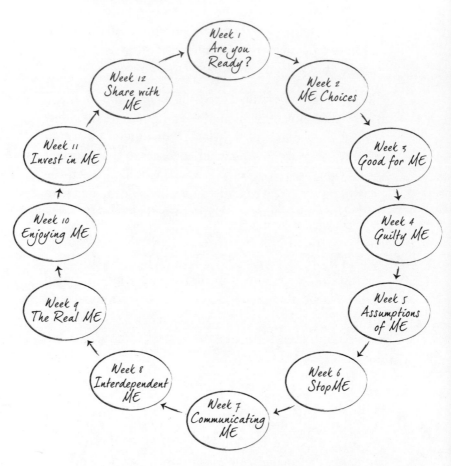

Your experience of this process will be unique, but it is best to start it when you are feeling well and able to cope, as your energy levels may dip through the process. Typically during the first three weeks, you will be energised, but the following three weeks can prove very draining and you will need to take extra care of yourself. During the final six weeks, your energy levels should build again.

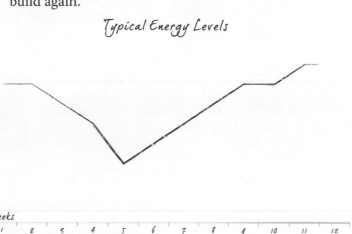

Typical Energy Levels

Weeks
1 2 3 4 5 6 7 8 9 10 11 12

Women's voices

I formally interviewed eight women MEs as part of my research and spoke informally to twenty others. Of the eight women, one was American living in the US and the rest were based in the UK. Those based in the UK were not all born there; while some were from Scotland, the North and South of England, others were from France, Jamaica and Africa. Their ages ranged from mid thirties to late fifties. Two were no longer married, all were in heterosexual relationships. They came to me through my work, friendships, chance meetings and online interaction. You will hear their uncensored voices extensively through this book in quotes and also have more in-depth stories of their unique experiences. I have anonymised their contributions and used aliases to protect their identities.

I chose to interview a small group of women because I wanted to understand and illuminate the uniqueness of how women MEs made sense of their lives. Even in this relatively small group, experiences and views are very different. Very much like children born to the same parents, their personalities, perspectives and experiences can diverge, even though their backgrounds are inherently the same. If I had taken a sample of hundreds, my fear is that the uniqueness and difference would have been drowned out by what was common to all, instead I wanted to give the difference a voice.

My hope is that even if your life, background, nationality, sexual orientation or heritage is different to these women, elements of their story will still resonate with you.

This is a practical and interactive guide with tried and tested transformational questions to reflect on and activities to undertake in every chapter. You will see them labelled with icons representing:

REFLECTION

or

ACTION

Your first step is to invest in a journal or notebook to capture your responses.

This book is not meant to be read and placed back on the shelf; keep it with you and let it guide you into becoming the best ME you can be.

Chapter 1 - Are you ready?

Through wisdom I have dived
down into the great sea,
And have seized in the place of her depths
a pearl whereby I am rich.
I went down like the great iron anchor, whereby men
anchor ships for the night
on the high seas,
and I received a lamp which lighteth me,
and I came up by the ropes
of the boat of understanding.

QUEEN OF SHEBA

As your guide I see it as my responsibility to ensure that you know how to equip yourself for your adventure through this book. In this chapter, I introduce you to the essential tools you will need: Reflection, Small Steps and Support. I help you to reconnect with what is important to you and why you would embark on this adventure in the first place through visiting your values and the impact of your happiness on others. Lastly, we ensure that your wellbeing and energy levels are right for you to start this adventure right now.

I am encouraging you to take a good look in the mirror and gaze with clear fresh eyes at what underpins your thinking and behaviour. This might be the first time you've really thought about being ME or it may be something you have long celebrated. Where you are in your thinking will affect what you take from it. It may be a reaffirmation of what you know in order to help you feel resourceful and build on what you have achieved, or it may bring some new realisations for you. Both are great places to start.

It's so easy for me to encourage you to examine all of the challenges and opportunities associated with being ME right now; I am not walking in your shoes - especially when you've taken the time to wear them in. I imagine that they're now comfortable and they go with everything; why would you replace them with new ones or question if they are right for you?

Rhonda sums up the challenge of being ME eloquently: "By being a working career woman or career mum, whatever you want to call it, I'm trying to get the best out of both worlds. I'm trying to be true to who I am, not to who other people want me to be or what I think people think I should be. And that is difficult and, you know, none of this is easy."

The idea is that you understand what informs your decisions, reflect on what's important to you and become more aware. From this place of uncensored honesty with yourself, you can start to design your best life as ME.

Take your time and work through the activities and spaces for reflection I have provided over the coming week; there is no rush, but there should be a rhythm, a movement, a continuous flow. You'll find some resonate with you more than others, but give them all a try.

If you find yourself getting stuck on one activity or reflection, sleep on it, note it and then keep moving and flowing through the process. You can always revisit it at the end of the book, or more likely a realisation will come to you as you work through the guide that eases that sticking-point for you.

The tools

Support

This book is definitely a helpful guide, but, while you peel away the layers you wear on daily basis - starting with that tailored overcoat - I would also recommend finding some additional support before you get as far as the underwired bra. That support could be your partner, a friend, family member or spiritual guide. I have found many professional women come to me in my capacity as a leadership coach to support them. They value the unique space for reflection and empathy, the fact that they are not judged and the focus on moving forward.

Reflection

Reflection is critical to the process. I know ... you reflect all the time, in bed, on your daily commute, in the shower, while exercising. But do you really? Do you really capture those revelations in the middle of an exercise class or out walking the dog? Do you write things down, whether in a book or on a blog, do you capture your thoughts and feelings in their stark reality and actually hear what you are saying to yourself? This is the place to express yourself, uncensored and in glorious technicolour.

You can reflect in the journal you have purchased. A couple of musts; you must do it regularly and you must read it back and, if possible, read it aloud. We speak, but for some reason we don't always hear ourselves. This process of reflection, of being curious and inquisitive about your situation, is what will make this process work and work well.

Reflection will reveal places in which you can make positive changes in your life, help you to develop new ways of doing things and become more aware of how to create the path that will work for you. When you are reflecting you are thinking with a purpose, questioning and inquiring into the way you do things in order to make improvements for the future. Julia Cameron, in her book *The Artist's Way*, recommends writing a stream of consciousness every day, which is all the thoughts that come into your head first thing in the morning before you speak to anyone. Others write in a journal just before bed. You will find your own rhythm.

I read recently that the American actor Tyler Perry used this type of writing to change his life. Writing enabled him to let go of his troubled past and start his career by sharing the stories of his experience through plays and movies.

If writing isn't for you, you have so many other options; you can draw, capture voice notes on a voice recorder, or create short video entries. One last thing; date your reflections, so that you can review the distance you've travelled.

 ACTION - Start Reflecting

Time to break in that new journal.

Set an alarm for 5 minutes' time so you don't have to disturb your flow by checking the time. Start reflecting now. Your focused question is: If you were to design your best life being ME what would it look like? Write for 5 minutes, not lifting your pen from the page, not checking for grammar or correcting yourself. Write in as much detail as possible from different perspectives. And when the 5 minutes is up read it back to yourself, aloud if possible.

REFLECTION

* What surprised you about the process?
* What was the theme that repeated itself in your writing?
* When you read what you wrote, what was your overriding emotion?
* What are you compelled to do as a result of this activity?
* How will you integrate more reflection in your life?

Small things make a difference

I am going to refer to making small actions and commitments to change throughout the book. When I say small things, I mean small: Things you can do today or tomorrow, with minimal effort that don't take much time; things that you *can* achieve. So if you come up with an action, break it down to the smallest possible action you can do to get it started and do it: This will be a catalyst for more small and successful actions. What is one small thing you can do by tomorrow to reflect more? Start now.

What's important to you?

You may be nervous about looking back, but we are only doing so in order to move forward. I know what it's like, we all bury our heads in the sand sometimes. But you know what? When you lift your head, your skin may be slightly exfoliated and younger-looking, but everything you were hiding from is still there. So let's face it together; you never know, there may be something to celebrate!

Maybe you haven't realised what you are not facing up to or celebrating in your role as ME:

* Can you talk about being ME without welling up with tears or showing red hot flashes of anger?

* Are you continuing as if nothing has changed, still doing everything you used to and now bringing in all the money too?

* Are you managing your life balance, feeling good about work, home and life?

* Are you proud and happy being ME and a role modelling success?

* How do you feel about maybe not being the one your child runs to when they need advice or comfort?

Whatever your responses, they will be lessons to learn from and experiences to build upon.

The first step to moving forward is: Understanding your past in order to see the present clearly and have a better future. I don't mean dwelling in the past and blaming others or getting caught up in the emotion of your past experience. The idea is not that you start confronting family members who teased you, or parents who didn't let you go to the party with your friends. That is all done now, let it go and... breathe! Although, if you do have some significant and serious issues that keep you stuck in the past, I recommend you visit a professional counsellor or therapist. What I am talking about is trying to understand how your past is impacting you now.

Those who have significantly influenced you in the past have helped to shape you. How much time have you spent thinking about who they might be? Some might call them role models. Professional women I have spoken to spend surprisingly little time thinking about it; however when they do, they are taken aback by who those people are. Sometimes it's their mothers, but more often, fathers, aunts, neighbours, people who they respected and were often self-made.

Your list of influences are having an impact on how you see the world now.

In the introduction, I told you a bit about my influences. The biggest influences for me have been my mother and grandmother and, understanding that my need to be responsible was both a blessing and a curse; changed the way I viewed being ME in my home. I know where my sense of responsibility and need to earn comes from, but actually things are not tough for me right now so I don't need to act as if they are. This is part of my story and I'm sure you have your own. When you are wise to it, you can gently shoo it away when it comes sniffing around, or embrace it like a long-lost friend who comes back into your life.

REFLECTION

* Reflect on your influences in your journal.
* Think of two or three people who have positively influenced you.
* List at least one thing that each of them taught you.
* How is what they taught you influencing your life now?
* How do you feel about that? Were you aware of how you felt?
* When you have finished reflecting, move on to the following activity.

ACTION - Values

Your values inform every decision you make, they are the rules by which you live and underpin who you are. Sometimes you can lose sight of them, particularly in times of stress. Reconnecting with what's important to you will remind you of where you came from and will help you make the right decisions for you as we go through this process.

On the next page is a table of values that have come up in my conversations with women MEs. You may think of others that resonate with you, if so please add them.

Examine each one carefully. What are your top 5? No one is going to see this, so be honest. You can circle them on the page or list them in your journal.

Give your reasons why. Are there any surprises? If so why is that? What does that mean for how you live your life as ME?

How can your values help you with the challenges of being ME?

Remind yourself of your values regularly. They are at the heart of who you are and help you to make the right decisions for you.

Table of Values			
Responsibility	Independence	Opportunity	Personal Development
Relationships	Self Awareness	Freedom	Power
Advancement	Achievement	Friendship	Family
Affection	Adventure	Health	Respect
Order	Cooperatio	Loyalty	Spirituality
Pleasure	Helpfulness	Wisdom	Wealth
Harmony	Economic security		

Awareness of ME

So you're ME, but do you even know how you feel about that? What about your partner, how do they feel? Who, or what, is influencing how you both feel?

Many of my conversations with women confirmed that their nerves are raw when their role as ME is discussed. One of my past leadership coaching clients described 'resentment' when she became ME and another, in an online discussion, described the time that she was ME as, "dark days" that she no longer wanted to remember, while others felt pride and achievement about their place in the world.

Andrea said, "I subconsciously just don't talk about any element of my work success. I would say I work mainly because it's interesting, it's never because 'it's financially lucrative, it's paid for the extension or its paid for the car' because I suppose it would make them question their own situation."

While Bernadette feels that, "Society hasn't caught up with women's need to be recognised as intelligent people, not just domestic people. I mean, you still have the role as a mum and still help around the house and still have a job. If you have a job, you know, it's almost a luxury at times because you still have a home to run."

A recent radio discussion described the male point of view when talking about stay-at-home dads. There was not one singular experience for men being at home; some loved it and even enjoyed being the token male in the playground with the 'yummy mummies' while others found it utterly soul-destroying.

With your life as ME often not outwardly accepted by society, no one would be surprised if you suppressed your true thoughts and feelings as a coping mechanism.

The process of raising your awareness can be unsettling. You've probably got some things buried away for a good reason; it could be painful, disruptive; mean change for you and others; but it could also make things better, more open and even easier.

Slow and steady should be your motto here. To start the process of raising your awareness gently, reflect on and write down your responses to these questions.

REFLECTION

* Did you have a choice in the way things are?
* Did you make the decision together?
* Is there a niggling thought or feeling that you are finding more and more difficult to ignore?
* Look at your responses, the language that you've used. The flow and the overall message - what does this tell you about where you are at with your thoughts and feelings on being ME?

ACTION

If you found the last reflection challenging and feel that you want to further unpack your feelings around being ME, then I recommend this focusing exercise. If you feel that you have reflected enough then you can skip this and move on to Happy ME on page 33.

You are so close to your situation that you may find it difficult to see it in a way that isn't charged with emotion. It is a real challenge to stand back and look at it objectively. I would like to introduce you to an approach called *Focusing*. It is a meditative approach to personal growth, which is underpinned by the belief that unresolved issues actually exist in our physical body. It has parallels with *Mindfulness*, which you may be familiar with. This short form *Focusing* exercise, created by Eugene Gendlin, can provide a space to listen to your body in order to gain answers you may not achieve by simply reflecting. (http://www.focusing.org/short_gendlin.html)

Let's try *Focusing* to help you unlock these feelings. Try it on your own first and then you may want your partner to support you or join in with you. Find a quiet space where you will be undisturbed for 20 minutes, preferably away from a desk and sit in a comfortable chair.

1. **Clear a space**

   How are you? What's between you and feeling fine?

   Don't answer; let what comes in your body do the answering.

   Don't go into anything.

   Greet each concern that comes. Put each aside for a while, next to you.

   Except for that, are you fine?

2. **Felt Sense**

   Pick one concern to focus on.

   Don't go into the concern.

   What do you sense in your body when you sense the whole of that concern?

   Sense all of that, the sense of the whole thing, the murky discomfort or the unclear body-sense of it.

3. **Get a handle**

   What is the quality of the felt sense?

   What one word, phrase, or image comes out of this felt sense?

   What quality word would fit it best?

4. **Resonate**

   Go back and forth between word (or image) and the felt sense.

   Is that right?

   If they match, have the sensation of matching several times.

   If the felt sense changes, follow it with your attention.

   When you get a perfect match, the words (images) being just right for this feeling, let yourself feel that for a minute.

5. **Ask**

   What is it, about the whole concern that makes me so

   _____?

   When stuck, ask questions:

   * What is the worst of this feeling?
   * What's really so bad about this?
   * What does it need?
   * What should happen?
   * Don't answer; wait for the feeling to stir and give you an answer.

* What would it feel like if it was all OK?
* Let the body answer
* What is in the way of that?

6. Receive

Welcome what came. Be glad it spoke.

This represents only one step on this concern, not the last.

Now that you know where it is, you can leave it and come back to it later.

Protect it from critical voices that interrupt.

Does your body want another round of *Focusing*, or is this a good stopping place?

As a result of *Focusing*, you are likely to have a new understanding, awareness or idea. Jot down anything that arose for you from the exercise as you will use it later.

Happy ME

I regularly buy a decaf soy latte when I am out and about. Occasionally, I will find that the seam of my paper cup isn't quite glued properly and my coffee is slowly seeping out. It's not obvious to the eye, but it is to the touch. I'll wrap it in a paper napkin, it absorbs it a little, but it doesn't go away. Just like the coffee, how you feel leaks out slowly, almost unobserved, but definitely felt.

It's an illusion to believe that you can feel miserable and it won't impact those around you. Just like your happiness, it has a ripple effect. You are part of a family unit, your happiness has far-reaching consequences. You owe it to those around you to be happy. Perhaps you won't recognise your impact until it's illustrated for you. Try creating your happiness map and see for yourself.

ACTION - Create Your Happiness Map

Drawing your happiness map will illustrate the extent to which you are making a difference to the lives of others. It will provide you with a clear picture of those who your happiness impacts most.

On the next page is an example of a completed happiness map; you can draw yours in your journal. Depending on the size, you may want to draw it over 2 pages.

1. Draw a circle with your name at the centre.
2. Draw lines extending outward from the circle and at the end of each line, write the name of someone you believe your happiness impacts. They could be: parents, partner, children, siblings, grandparents, grandchildren, aunts/uncles, neighbours, friends, colleagues, people you interact with on your daily commute to work.
3. Note how your happiness impacts them, e.g. when I wake up in a good mood, everyone has a good feeling in my home and they have a better day. When I smile at the postman on the way to work, he feels acknowledged and valued and hopefully, this has a knock-on effect on his day.
4. Spend a moment, look at this happiness map; a little bit of happiness can go a long, long way. Think about the converse; when you are unhappy it spreads the same distance, maybe further. Which map would you rather have?
5. What are the things that you need to address to ensure your happiness? You don't need to have the answers on *how* to address them just yet.

Olive's Happiness Map

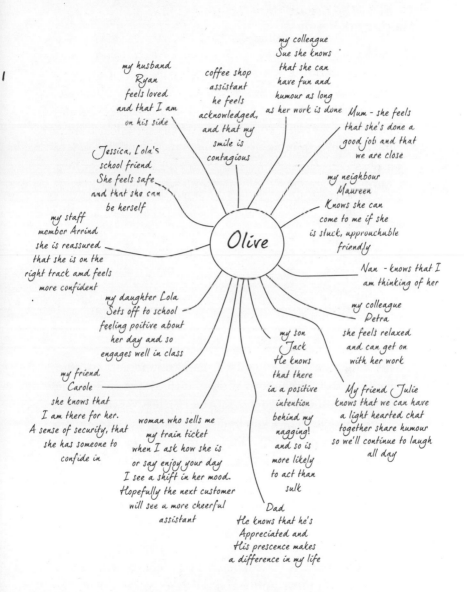

my colleague Sue she knows that she can have fun and humour as long as her work is done

my husband Ryan feels loved and that I am on his side

coffee shop assistant he feels acknowledged, and that my smile is contagious

Mum - she feels that she's done a good job and that we are close

Jessica, Lola's school friend She feels safe and that she can be herself

my neighbour Maureen Knows she can come to me if she is stuck, approachable friendly

my staff member Arrind she is reassured that she is on the right track amd feels more confident

Olive

Nan - knows that I am thinking of her

my daughter Lola Sets off to school feeling poitive about her day and so engages well in class

my colleague Petra she feels relaxed and can get on with her work

my friend Carole she knows that I am there for her. A sense of security, that she has someone to confide in

my son Jack He knows that there ia a positive intention behind my nagging! and so is more likely to act than sulk

My friend Julie knows that we can have a light hearted chat together share humour so we'll continue to laugh all day

woman who sells me my train ticket when I ask how she is or say enjoy your day I see a shift in her mood. Hopefully the next customer will see a more cheerful assistant

Dad He knows that he's Appreciated and His prescence makes a difference in my life

Wellbeing

Making ME happy

Nick Bayliss, in his book *A Rough Guide to Happiness,* says that one of the keys to happiness is balance. He suggests that to obtain happiness you need to do the opposite of what you usually do. So if you sit at a computer all day glued to your chair, you should do some physical activity in your downtime, such as dancing or karate. If you have a physically demanding role, you should do something more relaxing, like reading a book or listening to music in your downtime. It doesn't take much to regain this balance; twenty minutes of exercise could potentially balance out an eight hour day sitting at a desk. Do you usually measure the right balance in your life in terms of time? Twenty minutes of work doesn't mean that you need to find twenty minutes of family time to make up for it. You don't need to think of it in that way anymore, just work out what's right for you.

I would add that you also need to understand your feelings around happiness; do you think you deserve it, or is it for others who have more time, less responsibility, a charmed life? Have you been unconsciously sabotaging your own happiness? What's your story on happiness, is it short-lived, only for other people? Who do you know who seems happy? Identify what internal qualities help them to be this way.

Bernadette is now divorced, she has three children, one who still lives with her. She was born in France and moved to the UK when she was eighteen to work as an au pair, fell in love and stayed. While still married, her husband chose to stop supporting her and the children, even though he was still in full employment, so she was thrust into the role of financially - as well as emotionally - supporting the family.

"I mean definitely, I would never have been happy just being a housewife and mother because there was too much out there I wanted to find out, I wanted to learn, I wanted to do."

Few women admit to this. Being a wife and mother may just not be enough on your route to happiness. The world of work and career can offer an independent and different environment in which you can thrive.

I hope you are starting to feel curious about what really makes you happy. Here is an opportunity to begin to reflect on it, although you may have to keep asking yourself this question over a few weeks to get to the real answer and be honest with yourself.

REFLECTION

* What do you *think* will make you happy versus what *really* makes you happy?
* Be honest, when are you happiest?
* What's special about those times?
* How do others benefit when you are at your happiest?

Energise ME

I know that people have looked at me like I'm a lightweight when I've said that I have been travelling or training for a few days and need a day to recharge my batteries, but I am the one who is rarely ill; this is because I listen when my body is telling me to stop or slow down.

Andrea is a self-employed consultant and can usually manage her diary to be where she needs to be. She says,

"I work from home quite a lot, I'm kind of the common point, I can be around to do lots of things, so I end up doing most of them. But also I'm probably better at it than my husband because I do project management and he's not that way inclined."

You may recognise this, not just being ME, but also the home maker and 'go to' person for everything as well. This role at the centre of everything, pulled in many directions, can really take it out of you.

So how's your fuel? You need to be at least half full to embark on this journey, you don't want to break down on the way. Know what energises you and what depletes your energy and where your gauge is right now.

ACTION

One thing you can do to start to explore your energy level is log it. For one day, just log everything you do in your journal. Put the times down the left hand side and log hourly what takes place, also put an indication next to it, whether it energised or depleted your energy. You can create your own key. Try to make it a typical day, not when you're off on holiday or under extreme pressure. Here's an example of one ME's typical morning.

6am - make packed lunches 😕

7am - Shower 😕

8am - school run 😊

9am - commute - read book. 😊

10am - answered emails 😞

11am - one-to-one meeting with staff member 😊

12pm - writing report 😊

1pm - quick lunch 😐

When you have your log, reflect on the following questions in your journal.

REFLECTION

Looking at your typical day, what drains and what energises you?

Is there enough of what energises you? If yes, be happy. If no, what small action can you take to reduce what drains you and increase what energises?

Ask yourself, what will be better if you act now?

If you like, create a metaphor for that feeling, such as 'I feel light as a balloon when I plan to visit the gym one lunchtime a week'. You can then keep that metaphor as a reminder and ask yourself - 'Do I feel light as a balloon today?' If not you know you need to do something about your energy levels.

Temporary ME

Almost every woman I spoke to saw being ME as a temporary arrangement. I am not sure if this was a coping mechanism, 'It won't last forever so I'll just manage', or a true belief. Yes, it might be temporary, but it also might be permanent and treating situations as temporary puts you in limbo; is that where you want to be? Nothing is permanent or secure, but not taking action because things might change soon is not a helpful choice.

Perhaps you think that it's temporary because the pendulum swings for and against being ME many times on a daily basis. Rhonda is a successful businesswoman working in a male-dominated environment, she went back to work when her son was seven months old and, after discussions, her husband resigned from his job in order to be a stay-at-home dad. Strictly speaking, he is more than that, as he is going to be a property developer in order to further secure their future, but things are slow at the moment. When I asked her if it was a temporary arrangement, she said, "I would say it's for the foreseeable future, but sometimes I get quite irritated by the situation and I basically say to my husband, 'You're going to have to go back to work.' But it literally depends when you ask me that question as to what I think. Today, I think it's a foreseeable future thing."

Even if it is only temporary and things change shortly, don't you want your life to be the best it can be now? If you are viewing being ME as a temporary arrangement, you may want to reflect on why that is, using the questions below.

REFLECTION

How is thinking of being ME as temporary helping?

If you saw it as a permanent thing, what would you need to do that you're not doing now?

Sit with this knowledge and see where it takes you, without rushing into action.

Through this process of looking back, through understanding your past to see the present more clearly, you may be exhausted, a bit battle-worn, numb or have the effervescent feeling of excitement and energy. We've come a long way together. Through a series of actions and reflection you have explored:

* The fact that you are ME
* Who influenced you on your path here
* What the values are that govern your decisions
* Your feelings around being ME
* The positive impact your happiness has on others
* Your wellbeing and energy levels

Look at your notes in your journal, what do they tell you? Treat your notes with curiosity and let them propel you forward, they are the seeds of knowledge that you will grow and develop over the coming weeks.

Getting this far means that you have created the mental and physical space in your life to work through this guide. Are you ready to be the best ME you can be? If so, let's continue.

Chapter 2 - ME Choices

You always have a choice

Femi's story

Making my little corner of the world work

"My name is Femi. I am in my late thirties, married, and my husband works part-time. We've got two boys, five and six. To be honest, I think I've always been ME, because although we thought we'd end up earning the same amount it didn't turn out that way. He's always been laid back and I've always been a bit more driven. My parents were doctors and they instilled in me that I had to be professional. I am an accountant and have a senior management role, and yes, my parents are proud. I was born and grew up in Africa, while my husband was born in the UK and went back to Africa during his childhood. After we were married, we came to the UK.

Where does my drive come from? I grew up with a single Mum and she's always said to me, "You must work bloody hard," so in my head I am driven to work hard. Because my parents split when I was younger, being left desolate is a reality that I have witnessed. Whenever I meet people who are 'stay-at-home' mums and they are OK to completely depend on their husbands with no savings or back-up plan, I kind of look at them and think well, what if he leaves you? So I think one of my drivers is that there is no way I am not going to earn my own money.

I grew up with independence as a goal and my husband grew up in a family where mum doesn't work and his parents are still together, so he hasn't got the same insecurities about earning less or staying home that I do.

Did I make a choice to be ME? Well yes and no, I think it was more, 'You are going to work part-time because there's no way on earth I'm doing that.' When I have been a 'stay-at-home' mum for short spaces of time, I've been miserable due to lack of intellectual stimulation and then put too much pressure on the kids to fill the gap. Also in practical terms, we have a disabled son and the amount we need to spend in childcare ended up being the same as my husband would have been earning as his full-time salary, so he went part-time.

Now the boys benefit from having their dad around as he's much more able to deal with behaviour issues and is taken more seriously by the schools and the healthcare professionals than I am. This lifestyle is not typically African and my husband's had to deal with people questioning him and saying, "So you're the one doing the childcare?", but he - or should I say we - are managing it now.

You know, sometimes I think, if only you could turn it on and off. I would like to say to him, you work 24/7 for the next year and I stay at home much more and then we swap it around again. It seems there are times when it doesn't feel like a choice, although I realised early on that we had different benchmarks for how much was enough money and that I wanted so much more than him. I could have tried to change him into being more ambitious, but instead I am thankful that I could do it for the both of us.

For me, being ME is about making your little corner of the world work around your kids and constraints; you always have a choice in that."

ME perspective

It's interesting that you can come to the role of ME from many different directions: your partner could have experienced unexpected illness or redundancy; or there could be a significant age difference and your partner retired earlier than you do. Alternatively, like Femi, it could be just that you have more drive, determination and sense of wanting independence than your partner, or you've just found the work that you really want to do and it brings in a significant income. You may have uncovered some new realisation about this from completing the exercises in Chapter 1. How ever you've come to being ME, you have a choice whether to see it as a problem or find a way to make it work. It often involves seeing the world anew. If you have ever needed glasses you'll know what I mean: it's not until you get that new prescription that you realise what you've been missing. Things aren't fuzzy around the edges any more, they're crisp, sharp and focused.

How you *see* the world impacts how you *are* in the world

Femi didn't mention her siblings, but your position in your family often extends to the relationships you make later on in life. If you were the jester of the family in your childhood, you often carry on, being the funny friend or the partner who makes everyone laugh. If you've tried to step out of the role, people become uncomfortable with it because it challenges them to be different as well. So if you are the funny one, others can't be, they have to either be the one to laugh at your jokes or be labelled as having no sense of humour or fun. When major change occurs, like a partner becoming ill, you may need to change your role or take on others as well. This can lead to resistance from those around you as they need to change too. You may also find that the additional roles cause you to suffer from one or more of the following, as outlined by Carlson, Sperry and Lewis in 1997:

Role overload - when you have too many different and demanding roles. For example, being the perfect housewife and hostess is difficult to fit in with a demanding career.

Role strain - when the expectations of many different roles pull you in several directions at once. So you want to contribute your time to the parents' association but it means you will have to spend all day Saturday in the school hall, when what you really want to do is prepare the presentation for Monday's meeting and spend some time with the family. How do you meet all of those expectations?

Role conflict - when your roles are incompatible. There are times when your role can make it tough, for example you may choose to work nights and see this as a way to be there for the family and also maintain a career.

Noreen does just that, she works as a senior nurse, has three children and has been married for fifteen years. For many years she worked nights and then arrived home and took the children to school so that in her eyes, they wouldn't miss out. This placed great strain on her health and her marriage began to suffer. In the end, she had to take the decision to move back to working days, the roles were too conflicting.

ACTION - Family Relationships

Below are the family role types, outlined by Blevins in 1993, that adults seem to occupy. I think they are equally valid for looking at your home or work relationships. You will see there is a grid. You may want to draw this out in your journal. Have a look at the roles listed down the left hand side and tick those that resonate with you in the column marked 'Me'. Next, list the names of those closest to you in the other column headings, they could be in and outside work, and tick the roles that you think most sound like them in the appropriate column. You may also want to add some of your own role titles, if you think something is missing.

	Me	Partner	Work	Friend
Star Treated as special, performs at a high level, assumed to be quite bright.				
Blamer Blames others when things go wrong.				
Hero or Heroine Saves the day whenever anyone's in a tight spot.				
Rebel Doesn't quite fit in, autonomous, doesn't follow the rules. Dresses, thinks and behaves differently. Usually gets away with it.				

Martyr Endures suffering on behalf of others. Craves attention for doing this.				
Scapegoat Bears and accepts the blame when things go wrong.				
Distracter Takes focus away from problems or difficulties, finds other things to attend to.				
Cheerleader Stays on the sidelines and encourages others to take action. Not a risk taker.				
Jester Creates humour compulsively. Can be delightful and annoying.				
Invalid Sick, damaged, impaired in some way. Can take things on and not complete them.				
Appeaser Appeases people when things go wrong. Doesn't confront, passive.				

Oldest/favoured child Gets special treatment, takes responsibility for younger siblings.				
Mascot Kept around for good luck, cute, not expected to contribute much.				
Saint Never thinks, says or does anything wrong. Always behaves virtuously. Behaves as if they are better than others and people treat them as such.				
Sceptic Relied upon to cast doubt.				
(add your own)				

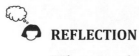

REFLECTION

When you have completed the table above, use the following questions to aid your reflection:

* What insights have you taken from completing this grid?
* How has this activity helped to bring your role as ME into focus?
* How does knowing the roles you take on impact how you feel about your choice in becoming ME?

* Are you experiencing role strain, conflict or overload? How do you know?
* Who in this grid can help you reflect on, manage, or generate ideas on making ME work for you?

ME attitude

Sometimes you don't exactly choose to become ME, but you can choose your attitude.

People inspire me every day through their attitude to adversity. Bernadette, who I mentioned in Chapter 1, has had it tough, bringing up three children on her own after her marriage failed and settling for work roles that didn't utilise her extensive knowledge and education. She is still ever hopeful: "I was quite strong in a way and I wanted to live my life. When I got married I wanted to be a wife and mother, depend on my husband, but that didn't happen so I had to really quickly pull my socks up and do what I could for my kids because there was nobody else. I was quite lucky, but I don't know if it's to do with me or if it's to do with the children. Having them, you know, they give me strength and you don't really feel sorry for yourself. I've got so much to do in my life, there are a lot of things I want to do with it. I'm not ready to retire or anything like that, not in the near future. If I can work until I'm eighty, I will work until I'm eighty!"

Bernadette had a choice; to feel beaten by her lot in life and spread toxic thoughts and emotions, but she has chosen to be positive, make the most of it and be hopeful.

What attitude have you chosen?

In his book *FISH!* a parable about finding the deep source of energy, creativity and passion that exists inside each of us, Stephen Lundin and his colleagues remind us that we always have a choice. He says: "There is always a choice about the way you do your work, even if there is not a choice about the work itself." And I say:

> **You** always have a choice about the way you engage in being ME, even if you feel there is not currently a choice as to whether you are ME for your family.

ME legacy

I asked all the women that I spoke to about the next generation; their children and beyond and how they might feel about women MEs. They recognised their role in shaping the future. Do you? How much do you think about the legacy you are leaving? Maybe legacy sounds too grand a title, you may prefer to think about the mark you leave on the world, but if you think about the impact of your past experience and those who have influenced you, you will be acutely aware of how important it is.

Whether consciously or unconsciously, you are creating a legacy. Here are just a few examples of how women like you are doing just that. Sally who has been ME in her family for twenty-two years, is married with two sons and a daughter. One of her sons was tasked with writing an assignment for school and it wasn't until he handed it in that he realised that he had cast the man as the home-maker and the woman as the one going out to work; reflecting his family situation.

Andrea has concerns of the media's current portrayal of men. She says ;"Men actually do get a bit of a rough time of it, or maybe it's just things that I'm reading, whereas the women seem to be increasingly characterised as smarter, doing it all and having it all. It's all very positive for the women and men are kind of made out to be a bit like this guy, just kind of sat at home, getting overworked who just doesn't see it all happening. And actually I'm more worried that I pick up on that and continue that - being a bit down on men with my son, so that I have to be very positive because I've heard myself talking about it as I'm talking to you. Going, 'Oh well women are more analytical and women are a bit more this and women are a bit more that.'"

Meanwhile Sondra, who has four girls, realised through talking to me that she is leaving a legacy of staunch feminists, surely their mum's drive, independence and accomplishment must have influenced that! You are not just influencing your children, but other women who watch and learn from you in the same way that you have been influenced by other women.

You are creating the future. If you haven't reflected on the legacy you leave, how you are a role model and influence others, this is a good time to start because how you choose to react to the role of ME has a significant knock-on effect.

REFLECTION

* How have you chosen to react to being ME?
* How is this view impacting you and others?
* If you carry on as you are, what is your legacy?
* How might you want to make that even better?

Feeling you have a choice

If you've ever tried to change someone else's point of view, you know that we can all be focused on how we see the world, so much so that we are actually quite blinkered. Knowing this means that changing yourself can be even tougher. It's easier to see what's going on with other people because you are on the outside; it's much tougher to look at yourself. But changing how you see things can lead to an increase in choice and opportunity. If you find yourself thinking that you are right, or not being open to hearing opposing views, perhaps you may have started to close down your ability to see others' perspectives. But others' points of view can enhance yours rather than diminish them. So you don't always have to lose something in order to embrace something else.

Connie did it, you can too. Connie is in her fifties, she is married and has worked her way up to a senior strategic position in education. She is an energetic, optimistic, highly educated woman. Her husband, who is very academic, was made redundant and as her career developed, his suffered a setback. Connie expressed some annoyance with her role as ME in the beginning, but has come to terms with it. She spoke about how lovely it was for her to be able to buy a brand new car recently without having to think about it. She is making the most of a choice that was thrust upon her.

The activity below is designed to be a catalyst for change. If you have a coach or trusted friend, you might find it helpful for them to guide through and probe your thinking, but if not, you can do it on your own. Just make sure you spend sufficient time at each stage really examining the world from that perspective.

This activity is based on a technique called Perceptual Positions which comes from Neuro Linguistic Programming or NLP, which you might be familiar with. NLP is an approach to communication, personal development, and psychotherapy; it's useful for considering new perspectives and ways of understanding and managing. This is one of the techniques that I introduce on the degree-level accredited coaching programme that I facilitate. When I use it as a tool in one-to-one coaching, clients have found it provides breakthroughs for them.

 ACTION - New perspectives

Give yourself twenty minutes to complete this activity fully, make notes in your journal from each position.

1st Position Self - Tell your story. How did becoming ME happen for you? In particular, focus on the aspect of your sense of choice. How you felt about it, your decision-making process, was it a quick decision or one you deliberated on, who was involved, etc.

2nd Position Other - Imagine your friend has just told you this story, what would your perspective on the story be? Particularly in relation to choice. What do you admire in the other person? What did you notice about the way they told their story? What insights do you have for them?

3rd Position Objective - Now imagine you are watching you and your friend talking. What would be your perspective on what was being said in regard to choice? Gut feelings: What's helpful about what you hear? As an observer, what do you see that they don't?

4th Position Universal - Finally, imagine you are outside watching someone watch you and your friend speaking about your story and your sense of choice; what does it look like now? What does this global view provide? What's interesting from this view? What's different about how you feel?

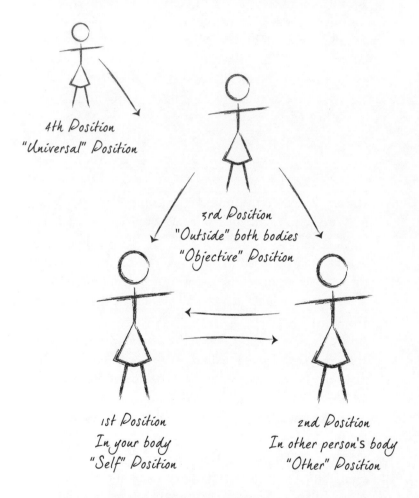

4th Position
"Universal" Position

3rd Position
"Outside" both bodies
"Objective" Position

1st Position
In your body
"Self" Position

2nd Position
In other person's body
"Other" Position

Completing this activity may have provided shifts and new ways of seeing things, now use the reflection questions to understand and learn from the process.

REFLECTION

* How did your feelings shift through each stage in the process?

* What do you notice that's different about how you see your sense of choice?

* If you are still finding it tough, challenge your perspectives, hold the opposite view to your usual one.

* What does your world look like from this place? What learning is there in this for you?

Don't hold back on your choices

Your inner critic has been sitting there closing down your thoughts and ideas for a while. Do you hear her softly whispering limiting thoughts in your head? For me it's a bit like being in a hundred metre sprint, I sprint off and about fifty metres on, my inner critic will kick in. She'll whisper in a low and concerned voice: 'You're not really a good runner, sports wasn't your thing at school, how can you expect to win now? Other people are fitter than you, their legs are longer, they've probably practiced so much more.' And suddenly, I realise I've stopped. I've talked myself out of it.

Tim Gallwey, in his book *The Inner Game of Work*, calls it our 'Interference'. Why let anything interfere with achieving your full potential?

If your inner critic wasn't whispering in her dulcet tones, what choices would be available to you? The way to stop listening to her is to focus on what you can achieve, using the example above. It would be good for you to visualise and stay focused on what you want to do, which in this case, is getting to the finishing line of a race, focusing on what you need to do to finish it and how you are going to do it, leaving no space for her voice. The more you make it real for you, the less doubts will creep in.

ACTION - Choices Star

If you've been thinking in a set way for a while, it's likely you'll believe that there are no more options open to you. This activity is designed to help you reopen and re-examine choices available to you.

In your journal, draw a star shape as large as you can on the page. If you have one, stick a photo of you in the centre, if not you can just write your name.

Add all the choices available to you, however wild and implausible they may be, as spokes on a star. Fill all the spokes on the star and create more if you need to. Here are some questions to prompt your thinking:

* What choices are available to you?
* What else could you be doing?
* How else could you be living?
* Who else could you be living with?
* How else could you organise your life?
* What other decisions could be made?
* What could you say that you haven't?
* What could you ask for that you haven't?
* Where else could you be working?
* How else could you be working?
* Who else could you involve in your life?

REFLECTION

Look at the star you have created. Do you have more choice than you thought?

Restore your sense of control

When becoming ME hasn't been your choice, restoring your sense of control in your life becomes really important. Even when it has been your choice, with so many plates spinning you can lose your sense of control and purpose. Designing your life in a way that works for you can be both exciting and overwhelming. I mentor women entrepreneurs and find that despite having many truly wonderful ideas, they are often stuck because they don't know where to start to shape their days and craft their life towards their vision.

Think about designing something, perhaps a dress for a special occasion. What are its qualities? Well it would fit you well, as it would be designed especially for you to complement your physique, it would be well-crafted, with attention paid to the tiniest details, perhaps even partly stitched by hand; it would be a one off unique piece showing off your personality. You may be living a vintage life that was not designed for you, so invest in a one-off designer life, that fits properly, works for you and shows off your assets.

Fearful of standing out from the crowd in this statement piece?

This extract from Marianne Williamson's poem speaks to the fear inside all of us:

"Our deepest fear is not that we are inadequate. Our deepest fear is that we are powerful beyond measure. It is our light, not our darkness that most frightens us. We ask ourselves, who am I to be brilliant, gorgeous, talented, fabulous? Actually, who are you *not* to be?

... Your playing small does not serve the world. There is nothing enlightened about shrinking so that other people won't feel insecure around you. We are all meant to shine, as children do.

... It's not just in some of us; it's in everyone. And as we let our own light shine, we unconsciously give other people permission to do the same. As we are liberated from our own fear, our presence automatically liberates others."

This poem speaks to the huge untapped potential within you. Imagine that it is fear of success or happiness that is holding you back. I encourage you to let go of fear, let your light shine.

ACTION - Moving away from fear

To move away from fear you need to move towards something, this activity is crafted to help you do that:

First step - Write a list of the skills, qualities and attributes that enable you to make good choices. If you find it difficult, think of compliments you often receive or ask for feedback.

Second step - Plan how these skills, qualities and attributes can help you move from fear to excitement.

Third step - Decide what is needed in your life to shift from excitement to optimism.

ACTION - Define your pioneering spirit

See how far you've travelled, fear is in the distance now.

You have complete freedom, unlike motherhood or being a wife, there is no roadmap for you as ME, you have the freedom to start from a blank sheet. How liberating is that? The ideal for you is yet to be realised, and so you have the power to create and define it in a way that makes sense for you.

This is more than your values, it's words that sustain you on the untrodden road. Look at the words on the next page. What defines your pioneering spirit as ME?

What one word would you like to hold with you to anchor you on this creative and pioneering journey of being ME?

Choose one word that you know will keep you going, write it in your journal and let it take up a whole page on its own. Give it space and room to be.

Words to define your pioneering spirit

pioneer   tenacious   caring   explorer

    fierce   resilient   developer

guide   leader   pilgrim   chief

    innovator   pathfinder   trailblazer

commander   counsellor   dignitary   equality

    conductor   dean   director

luminary   pacesetter   skipper   kindness

    manager   shepherd   independence

fairness   chieftain   service

    founder   lioness

Gosh, are you awash with choice?

Consider how you felt at the beginning of this chapter about choice. I am hoping that through the process of action and reflection, you are now seeing new perspectives on the choices you have and also the impact your attitude has on those who matter to you.

Knowing how important it is that you accept the choices you have made, or that have been made for you, is critical, but so is feeling that you have a choice in your future. With your enhanced perspective on your choice, you should have a restored sense of control, which is a great position from which to explore what's good about you being ME.

Chapter 3 - Good for ME

What's good about being ME

Don't be in a hurry to swallow when chewing is pleasant

NYANJA OF MALAWI PROVERB

It's easy to notice what's going wrong in your life, but think about what's going right. In my work delivering leadership training to groups of leaders, a question I often ask is: "When was the last time that someone told you that you were doing a good job?" Usually, only a few hands are raised, amounting to a small percentage of the group, but when I ask: "When have you been told that you didn't get something quite right or improvements needed to be made?" a sea of hands are all waving at me. We appear to live in a society where we find it easier to criticise than compliment, it doesn't help matters that when people receive a compliment, particularly in western society, they don't accept it with open arms, instead they often brush it off or dismiss it in embarrassment.

Unfortunately, this attitude ends up transcending work and affects the way you think about all aspects of your life, so that when you are thinking about your day, you look at it from a place of deficit, asking yourself: What's missing? What's not right? What do I need to fix?

Even if you see yourself as an optimist, how much time do you spend celebrating what's going right for you? What could you savour and appreciate more about your life?

There are so many things going well for you right now; being ME gives you a sense of control over your life, financial independence, a significant voice in your relationships and a bright future in which you can learn from experience and leave a legacy as well as, I am sure, much, much, more. Let's reflect, appreciate and savour the good for once.

Being ME, in control

Control for some can mean to have power over something or someone in a negative way, or to manipulate. What I mean when I talk about control is that you feel that you have some input into the way your life runs and that you are able to make effective choices and manage your life. So if the word control doesn't sit comfortably with you, swap it for a word or phrase that does. You're in control after all!

You may think of being in control as something that is performed alone, for example, 'I am in control', but I wonder if you've stopped to think about what is added in terms of value to your sense of control by those closest to you? You may be relying on them for support with childcare or the household chores; this support adds to your sense of being in control because you know that aspect of your life is sorted out.

Being able to make your own decisions can be a key part of feeling that you are in control. The women I spoke to all appreciated being in control as a result of being ME. Sondra describes one of the advantages of being ME. Her relationship with her husband is one of supportive equals, she knows that her husband Rick has no interest in holidays, she describes him as a 'homebody'. Her income and the fact that she works hard means that she can have an equal influence on the family priorities and can request that the family take a well-earned break together, which has resulted in regular holidays. Her husband wouldn't have necessarily wielded his power if the roles were reversed, it just wouldn't have been so high on his agenda.

Reflect on your sense of control through being ME. What's good about it?

REFLECTION

* How else do those around you support your sense of control?
* What else do you need to be thankful for that aids your ability to manage your life effectively?
* What decisions can you make as ME that you may not have done otherwise?

Financial independence

As I said in the introduction, the income is a trigger, a catalyst and a cause for many other things that you have to manage as ME, so it may not be the most important thing, but let's not deny it exists. Having your own money is great, you don't need to ask for money for purchases, or justify why you need that gorgeous new-season handbag or the latest gadget to make your life easier. My experience of meeting financially independent women is that they exude confidence, poise and self-reliance. The fact that you are used to being able to make decisions, that you know your own worth and you are doing well in your career, shines through.

Financial independence gives you power; you may shy away from the thought or you may rub your hands in glee. Either way, power is everywhere and not necessarily a bad thing; your boss has power due to her position, however you may hold the power when she needs something done that only you can deliver. Your financial independence means that you are not dependent on your partner for your economic security, although I am sure you will be dependent on them for some things.

Be careful not to wield this power over others, you should still make choices about how you use and manage money together, you are part of a family unit after all. Of course, all situations are different and how you manage your money will depend on this. Sondra says that she and her husband have a joint account and, as all purchases come out of it, they don't discuss whose money it is. Victoria holds separate bank accounts from her husband and thinks that's the safest option for her, whereas, in Connie's relationship, her husband manages all the finances, because he's always done it and is good at it. One woman I spoke to recalled how her mother was the main earner for many years, her father paid the essentials while she used her money for the luxuries like holidays and eating out, the higher her income the more luxurious lifestyle they led. Other women I have spoken to manage their own money and have a small amount in a joint account, it all depends on the situation. Sondra's advice to all women is save, save, save, as who knows what tomorrow will bring.

One thing that is clear, you won't be with your partner because you need them financially, you will be with them because you want to be, which is a great positive for any relationship.

In your bid to be fair and equal and not disempower your partner, you might steer away from the subject of money altogether. Burying the subject away is not what I would advise, instead try understanding your attitudes to money. This will enable you to make important decisions such as: who manages it, what purchases and investments you make and how you will build your future.

The activity below is not just for those who have never approached the subject of money in their relationship. This activity provides you with a new language to consider your current approach and review it, even if you feel that it is already working for you.

 ACTION - Broaching attitudes around money

I have completed an example for you. You will need to draw your own axes in your journal and add your own X's when you have considered which quadrant you and your partner should belong in.

You may have a particular situation that is influencing your thoughts at the moment, such as an impending potential redundancy or you may have just received a tax bill, but try to think of yourself as you typically are.

Attitudes around Money

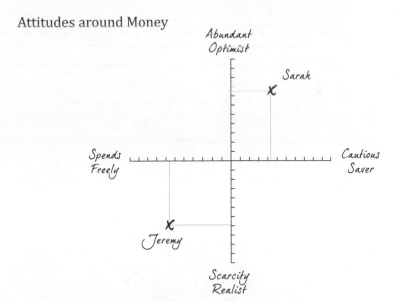

When you have drawn your axes, first think about the horizontal axis entitled 'spends freely' and 'cautious saver', which side are you on?

Spend Freely - If you consider yourself impulsive, intuitive or spontaneous when it comes to money, you would mark yourself highly on this axis. You are the type of person who would arrive home one day with a brand new car because you saw it and liked the colour; it was, in your opinion, a bargain or you just wanted the latest model. If the money is there you don't think twice about spending it.

Cautious Saver - If you consider yourself to be someone who always saves rather than spends or invests, you are likely to mark yourself highly on this axis. The thought of having this financial cushion of savings helps you sleep at night. You will weigh up the pros and cons of any spending carefully. A large purchase like a car would require a considerable amount of research and you would not take any risks, you would also think very carefully about justifying your need for a new car in the first place. Your cautiousness may mean that you wait before purchasing to see if items are discounted or even if you'll have a job next month.

Mark yourself on the axes depending on where you see yourself, so the further towards the 10, the stronger you feel about your affinity with it. In the example, Sarah marked herself low on the cautious saver, as she felt that she didn't spend freely. Although she likes to save, she can be impulsive with money on the odd occasion.

When you have marked that go to the second axis.

Next think about the vertical axis entitled 'abundant optimist' and 'scarcity realist', which side are you on?

Abundant Optimist - If you consider yourself to have a motto something like, 'Don't worry, there'll always be more money,' you would mark yourself highly on this axis. You may not be sure where it will come from, but feel sure the universe will provide for you. Your expectation is that there will always be enough, that money will just keep coming. You are willing to invest in something that seems like a good deal, even if you have to borrow the money, as you anticipate it will come good in the end.

Scarcity Realist - If you consider yourself to be someone who thinks that there will never be enough money then you would mark yourself highly on this axis. Even though you have savings in the bank, you want to act carefully and frugally, spending as little as possible, anticipating hard times. You need a very valid reason to spend any money and would be more likely to deprive yourself of something others would think essential.

Mark yourself on the axes depending on where you see yourself, so the further towards the 10 the stronger you feel about your affinity with it. In the example Sarah marked herself high on the abundant optimist, because even though she is cautious with money and likes to save, she feels there will always be more.

You then draw 2 lines - which are dotted on the above example - and mark an x where they cross each other.

Now have a conversation with your partner about where you are and ask them, where do *they* sit?

Are you the same or different?

If you and your partner are in different quadrants: without trying to change their attitude, discuss the tension that can be caused by differing views and also what having different views brings to your relationship.

When you and your partner are in the same quadrant: again without trying to change their attitude, discuss what's good and also potentially limiting about this.

You both now know where you are coming from, you can both make decisions to change.

An interesting thing to do is ask your partner to mark where they would have put *you* on the graph and vice versa, because our partner's perspective can be quite different and this will give you an insight into how you come across regarding money.

Here is a brief description of each of the quadrants; you should illuminate them by discussing your situation fully, rather than by thinking about them in isolation.

Cautious saver and abundant optimist - is careful with money, a good saver and cautious investor, but believes even if they lost it all, they would accumulate it again.

Cautious saver and scarcity realist - is careful but also believes that there is never enough money and never will be.

Scarcity realist and spends freely – spends today and worry's about it soon after, feeling regretful for not being more cautious.

Abundant optimist and spends freely - believes in spending for today, as there will be more tomorrow.

 REFLECTION

How can you build on what's working in terms of your finances?

Be gentle with your partner's feelings here

ME voice

Being ME can mean that your voice is heard when it normally wouldn't be. As you are acutely aware, being

ME has been traditionally associated with men and it meant that their voice was heard. Andrea views being ME as playing an important part in equalising relationships: "We've both been on fairly equal salaries since we got married so we do have a very equal footing, compared to some of my friends where the man is the main breadwinner, I'm amazed by the lack of influence they have on the decisions or the things that may not be discussed. My old school friend's husband was going for another job and they were expecting their third child, the new job would have meant that her husband was away from home for three or four weeks at a time and she was saying, 'How on earth am I going to cope?' But she hadn't had that conversation with her husband and she was saying to us, 'Well I can't ask him not to do it,' and I was saying to Ralph, 'How on earth can she not be talking to her husband about that?' He said, 'Yes, but she won't be the main breadwinner and if he's bringing in the money and they want a better life, that's probably why she's keeping quiet,' and then we didn't discuss it again and the penny dropped for me."

You are in the strong position of having what you say listened to; make sure it's worth hearing. So you've got a voice, how are you using it? Here are some questions to help you reflect on that.

REFLECTION

* How do you make decisions about large purchases?
* Does one person's voice have more weight in your relationship? If so, why is that?
* Who makes decisions regarding the children?
* If either of you wants to change the way they work how would you make that decision?

* There is no right or wrong, but if you find that your voice is loudest on everything or vice versa, you might want to consider if this is right for your partnership.

* How does this translate into the workplace, how does being ME inform whether and how you voice your opinions?

The future looks bright for ME

You are learning all the time. Taking the road less travelled means that you have to learn as you go. A male client of mine said to me once: "Some people live and learn and some just live." It stuck with me; which group could you be in? If you are in the group that live and learn, this quote from Peter Senge's book *Presence* should resonate with you: "People with a high level of personal mastery live in a continual learning mode. They never 'arrive'. Sometimes, language, such as the term 'personal mastery' creates a misleading sense of definiteness, of black and white. But personal mastery is not something you possess. It is a process. It is a lifelong discipline. People with a high level of personal mastery are acutely aware of their ignorance, their incompetence, their growth areas. And they are deeply self-confident. Paradoxical? Only for those who do not see the 'journey is the reward'."

If you're not doing so, should you spend some time learning from your experiences?

How do you learn? In Chapter 1 we introduced the importance of reflection and I have been prompting you to do this in your journal ever since. Even so, perhaps you are not sure what you are actually learning. A useful way to reflect on your experience and learn from it is to create a timeline.

ACTION - Your ME Timeline

This is an opportunity to look back over the period you have been ME, and learn from the highs and the lows and take these lessons to make things even better. It will also help you review how far you've travelled.

I've drawn one here for you. I suggest you use a page in your journal to create your own.

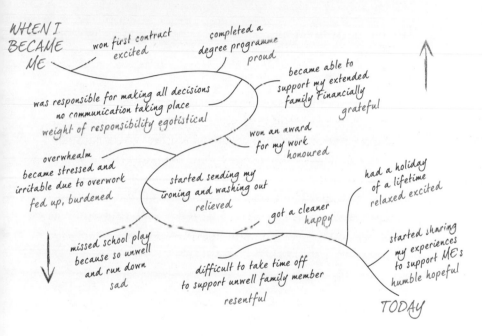

Draw your ME timeline in your journal. I suggest you draw it landscape.

Make the start date when you first became ME and the end date now.

Mark key moments of professional and/or personal significance in chronological order.

Put those that you recognise as positive above the line and those that were more challenging below the line.

Note if these were instigated by yourself or by others.

What was your overriding emotional response at the time? E.g. fear, excitement, sadness, joy, anger etc...

How do you view that key moment now time has passed?

What learning are you taking away from these experiences?

What small actions will you put in place as a result of the learning from this activity?

The legacy we leave

We have seen the future, and it wears skirts

BILL KRIGE, SOUTH AFRICAN JOURNALIST

OK, perhaps in the future, we may not *all* wear skirts, but women are definitely leaving a legacy. According to recent research, many of us will be living to one hundred years old, so we have many years to make an impact. We will be influencing the next generation and watching them grow. The hope is that there will be no stigma, whether you are a stay-at home-dad or a female ME, all the women I have spoken to expressed this wish.

Sally's children stayed home with their dad, he is an artist and her two sons both have artistic leanings. She also had a daughter who is much more practical, like her. Femi expressed concerns that her children might lack ambition because they saw their dad at home. All of the women that I spoke to wanted their children to have a choice to live their lives in the way that suited them, whether that meant having one main earner of either gender, or just creating the lives that would work for them.

You are not the only role model. Your partner will have an influence and those who your family come into contact with, such as educators, religious leaders, neighbours, family and friends. But what you do does make a difference. Sally described it as, 'showing her children how to go out into the world.'

Remind yourself what's working. You are making a difference; there are an increasing number of women on boards, more women CEOs, and a burst of women entrepreneurs working on their own terms. Progress is being made one step at a time.

 ACTION - 3 Questions

Working from the back page of your journal, just before you go to bed each night, reflect on these 3 questions every day for 30 days:

1. What have I learnt?
2. What improvements can I make?
3. What am I thankful for?

This process of beginning a pattern of learning every day will incrementally improve your life and begin to develop "personal mastery".

We've explored control, financial independence, having a voice and learning as being the positives about being ME.

Take a moment to breathe and reflect on what's really good for you about being ME.

Compliment yourself on getting here and all your achievements.

Enjoy and savour this moment in whatever way feels right - well done.

Chapter 4 - Guilty ME

Stop being so hard on yourself

You can outdistance that which is running after you but not what is running inside you.

RWANDAN PROVERB

One of the internal battles that you may be facing is one with guilt - torn between children, career, elderly relatives and your partner. This guilt serves no purpose other than to constantly drain your energy. If you are always thinking about where else you should be or what else you should be doing, you are not giving your full attention to now. This means that generally, the quality of your interactions with those closest to you diminishes. The guilt eats away at you in the form of *wishes*: I *wish* I could be at home for my elderly mother in case she has a fall; I *wish* I could be with my child all day instead of waving goodbye at the nursery gates; I wish I could give more to work; if only I could spend a couple more hours working on that pitch I know I could win the business. You know what? It is what it is, and the guilt of not doing what you think you should be doing is stealing precious time away from you.

I wonder what feeds your guilt? Is it your upbringing, your spirituality, your religious belief, the company you keep? Start craving other forms of nourishment.

Give a yes or no answer to these questions:

Does guilt help you?

Does it enhance your relationships?

Does it guide you positively?

I hazard a guess that the answer is no to all three questions. In fact, I guess that it's slowly eating away at all that could be enjoyed in your life. Sounds like a bold assertion. Think carefully, can you really disagree?

By now guilt is an essential accessory for you, like an invisible handbag that you carry around all day. You no longer remember picking it up but sometimes you feel those straps digging deeply into your shoulders. Find a way to rest this bag on the floor or, better still, put it to the back of the closet, and everyone will be happier.

Guilt-informed decisions

Do you own your sense of guilt or project it onto others? What you think others want and need from you may not be accurate. I am sure that you know a parent whose child kicks and screams when parted from them, only to be playing happily within minutes of them turning their back. Guilt can be a lot like that, you feed it with your imagination, visualising a child screaming unhappily, yearning for you all day when actually they are getting on with their life in your absence. Your wishes are not necessarily their wishes, you are feeding the beast with your guilt.

From this place of wishing and imagining, you can make poor decisions, like thinking you need to be at home for the children when actually you know that this would be unfulfilling for you. You become the martyr. Remember the family relationship grid that you completed in Chapter 2, when you can slip into the role of self sacrificing mother, daughter, partner, colleague and friend? This role is no good for anyone because as the martyr, you expect respect and rewards for self-sacrifice and it is likely that you won't get any. There is a ripple effect; you become resentful and despondent and even more unhappy and then become guilty about that. So the ripple continues, waves of guilt, guilt and more guilt.

I have a prime example. Mira is a teacher in her late fifties, she works full time and looks after her mum, she has been married twice. Unfortunately her relationship broke down with her ex-husband around four years ago, but she continues to be a single ME now looking after her mum. Rather admirably, she spends her out-of-work time with her, which she says is to stop her mum feeling lonely. Her mum spends her days dozing and listening to the radio and is increasingly despondent. Why would Mira leave a fulfilling job informing young lives to be with someone who hardly interacts with her? Love is part of it, but guilt is really the answer. What will happen if she stops doing it? No doubt the ripples of unhappiness and guilt will begin.

In order to let go of guilt, you need to replace it with something better. Well, how about trust? Trust that those around you are resilient, I haven't met an adult who said that they recall being sent to nursery too early and very few parents really want their children to give up their lives for them or to be unhappy and unfulfilled doing so.

Trust that for others to be happy you don't have to be unhappy.

The thing is, you could let guilt steal all of your time and start to become acutely sensitive to the comments of others. Victoria is in her early forties, she has been married for eleven years and has one child, she has been ME all of her married life, her husband works, but over the last four years the gap in their incomes has grown.

Victoria loves her work. She has a friend, Tricia. They met at a baby group when their children were only a few months old. Victoria went back to full-time employment when her daughter was about a year old while Tricia has been the homemaker over the last ten years. Victoria said: "Whenever I talk to Tricia about the work I really enjoy, she says, 'poor thing'. At first it used to lead me to think that I was indeed a 'poor thing', but when I looked at it more closely I realised that my child and I were not missing out and that actually the choices I was making were the best ones for me."

If Victoria had chosen to feel guilty for not being a stay-at-home mum, what purpose would that have served? Perhaps it would dilute the time she did have with her child by making her worry about what she should be doing.

Entrusting ME

One of the realisations that it is important for you to come to is that you can't do it all, you must entrust some of your other roles to those around you and not feel guilty about that decision. Rhonda has some flexibility in her role and is able to work from home sometimes. She described trusting her husband to do a good job: "This morning he was giving Alex his breakfast, Alex is particularly whiney at the moment because of his teeth and I could see Tom getting very short-tempered. Because this is yet another day that Alex is being like this. At times like that he realises it's a lot more difficult than most people think."

Maybe you would have wanted to step in at that point. Why? If you have left your child in safe hands and you are on the premises, how guilty should you feel? Or is it assumptions about your role: I am the mum, I must do the caring? Checking your child would have undermined your partner and also removed your focus from work. In addition, you would have found it even harder to tear yourself away. The advantage of working from home is that you don't have to travel and can spend more quality time with the family. It doesn't mean that you need to take over. Sometimes you may worry and feel guilty when it is not your place to do so. Have you given over the role as carer and home manager in word but not necessarily in deed?

ME buttons

Guilt that is stealing your precious time and energy will be noticeable to others. It will leak out in the form of one or more of the following: short temperedness; being unwell; negativity and the way you look and hold yourself. Have you ever worked out what someone's triggers are? The things that you can say or do that can push their emotional buttons? I am sure you know which buttons to press for those closest to you.

There is a button called 'guilt-trip' hidden on you somewhere. Sadly, those closest to you know where to locate it and can push it the hardest. Kids are great at knowing what buttons to press. Don't fall into the trap! You'll end up compensating for being ME over and over in all sorts of ways if you do, and they will never be the right ways. The work environment can be a competitive place, don't let guilt be your Achilles heel.

Unchecked, your guilt can become the centre of everything. The heart of all problems and issues that occur in your life e.g. my child is being bullied at school, my father is in the hospital, it must all be because I am ME. If you let it take hold, it will become the centre of all family arguments, creating a seed of resentment that grows and grows. It may be doing so already. Do you recognise it?

You have the ability to step back and look at your situation objectively. When you do so, there is no space for guilt - only what is and what do you want it to be? Below is an activity to help you do this.

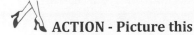 **ACTION - Picture this**

Imagine watching yourself through a TV screen, or on your tablet computer; you are on the outside looking in. Being played on the screen is a typical working day in your life. You have a remote control and can press play, fast forward, rewind and freeze-frame.

1. Start watching this typical day, fast forward to the decisions you make, rewind them and review them until you have think you have observed enough.

2. How does your decision-making look from the

outside?

3. What do you notice about your sense of guilt that you are usually too close to notice? How is guilt impacting your decisions?

4. What grain - or should I say pixel - of truth are you now more aware of?

Risky ME

Thankfully you are not alone, you are part of a unique, richly diverse family system. Your guilt will make a difference to how your system works and interacts, just as your happiness will.

Thrashing yourself with dry twigs every day, while good for boosting the circulation, will place you in the position of fighting yourself or giving in, usually appearing to those around you as anger or defeat.

What is done can be undone - it's never the end of the world.

REFLECTION

How risky is it to let go of being hard on yourself for a while?

One of the activities that I carry out with groups of leaders to help them take their leadership performance to the next level involves asking them, after they have completed a competitive activity, to decide whether to stick with what they have achieved so far or risk their performance for another chance at improvement. It always surprises me how many groups stick with where they are at, even when there's nothing to lose. This excessive caution prevailing in the workplace says to me, 'I would rather not try than get it wrong.' This approach can stop you tapping into ways to make things radically better!

How risky is it to let go of things that you think you should be doing? How risky is it to tell your children that you really enjoy work and that it's a part of you so you're not going to feel bad about it?

How risky is it to say that you enjoy the financial reward and status that being a successful and accomplished woman brings?

What's more, if you're being tough on yourself, it's likely you are also being tough on those around you. Would you want to treat others the way you are treating yourself? When you stop being hard on yourself, you give others permission to do the same.

Ever thought to yourself: 'If life's hard for me, why shouldn't it be hard for you?' How helpful is this way of thinking? Is that what you want for those closest to you?

Find ways to relax yourself, the reins, the intensity... breathe.

What's the real risk in letting go of feeling guilty? Try it and see how it works out for you.

 ACTION - Tummy Breathing

One of my favourite techniques for letting go, because of its simplicity and effectiveness, is called tummy breathing. It's perfect for reducing stress and calming your thoughts. Download full instructions from www.rockingyourrole.com

Share the responsibility

You are definitely a capable woman, being ME is a feat on

its own. Running a successful family, keeping abreast of school trips, family birthdays, maintaining a home and a career, requires considerable project management and people skills. But you are definitely not going to be the only capable person in your household. What do those who you share your home and life with bring? Utilise others' skills and talents.

Remember, as I said in Chapter 4, decisions don't necessarily need to be made by you alone. Share the load and it will alleviate the guilt as it will no longer all be your responsibility.

Being ME doesn't mean you are the sole decision maker and the carrier of all burdens. Just because you might not share the financial load doesn't mean that you can't share areas.

Let it go. Beating yourself up puts you in a position of fighting yourself or giving in. Constantly battling yourself will derail your career and make you unwell. I have met women who describe their time being ME as the worst period in their life, they found it too stressful and couldn't manage, they weren't supported and so it is a time they would rather forget. The weight of this role can give you unbearable pressure if you choose not to let go of the guilt that can be associated with it.

This discomfort could be a nagging pain in the head or an ache in the shoulder; listen to your body and let it tell you what's going on. You may be familiar with the work of Louise Hay, in her book *You Can Heal Your Life*, she describes how your body has a lot to tell you about how you are feeling.

Your career is important, the way you feel about life can derail what happens inside the workplace. When you're at work that is where your focus needs to be. Ensure that you are organised, so that if a meeting overruns you don't end up dashing out because the nursery will charge you a pound a minute if you're late. I have attended meetings with women in senior roles and seen them appear downtrodden and worn out. It's not a good look. How is your guilt showing itself at work? If you don't look and act like you really want to be there, you will be passed over for promotion in favour of someone who is hungry and enthusiastic. Is this what you want?

Light and shadow

Giving in will mean that you are defeated - who wants to be around someone like that?

We all have a shadow side, the place we go to in times of stress. If you are an outgoing person, this might be the time that you shut everyone out, or you might be someone who prides themselves on being calm and collected and find yourself becoming much more emotional. Understand your shadow, where you go to in times of stress and pressure. Recognise triggers and be aware. This excerpt from *Coming Home to Myself*, written by Marion Woodman and Jill Mellick, may help you reflect on this:

"When we stand in the light, we cast a shadow. Light and shade are to each other as breathing in is to breathing out. Some aspects of ourselves are in the light, visible to us and others. Other aspects, positive and negative, are in shadow, unseen by us, even when seen by others. These are parts of ourselves that have been neglected, disowned, forgotten, judged, unrecognized, or undeveloped.

Some of the ways we can glimpse what is in the psychological shade include: noting what we idealise or denigrate in others; recognising our uneasiness about others' perceptions of us (good and bad); and paying attention to our bodies, where shadow can sometimes reside as a physical symptom (an aching back, a pain in the stomach).

Our shadow is an infinite reservoir of energy. Learning to recognise and to take responsibility for our shadow qualities gives us more choice in responding consciously and creatively to the possibilities life offers us.

The shadow is anything
we are sure we are not;
it is part of us we do not know,
sometimes do not want to know,
most times do not want to know.
We can hardly bear to look.
Look.
It may carry the best of the life
We have not lived."

REFLECTION

* If you are demonstrating that life is a burden that must be endured, is that the message you want to give out?

* When in your waking hours do you not feel guilty?

* What small steps can you take to extend that time?

Develop resilience

People are like plants in the wind: they bow down and rise up again.

MALAGASY PROVERB

How can you choose to be?

A better use of your energy would be to develop resilience for a time when the world comes battling. Resilience is about bouncing back, it's not about being so tough that you don't fall in the first place. Rather than feeling guilty, replace it with a sense of resilience. Your ability to bounce back is an important skill. You are flexible and adaptable in your approach and are sure to be demonstrating resilience as ME.

It's easy for me to say let go of guilt, but how do you do it? Here's an approach to putting all of this into practice and letting go of the guilt associated with being ME.

ACTION - Guilt free ME

1. Choose two images that you like, they can be from magazines, books or images from the internet - don't choose images that you already have some relationship with, like your favourite artwork or family photos.

2. Use image 1 to articulate guilt by saying or writing, *this image defines my guilt by...*

3. Use image 2 to articulate your world free from guilt, by saying or writing, *this image defines my guilt free life by...*

4. Notice what was different about your energy, pace, types of language used and emotions when you articulated how the images defined your life.

5. Throw the image which defines your guilt away, choose to live the guilt-free life today.

6. Stick image 2 in your journal to remind you.

Are you feeling lighter now? You should have a bounce in your step. If you weighed yourself before and after working through this chapter, I think you would have lost a few pounds of guilt. Now you've just got to keep it off, keep reminding yourself how the guilt was holding you back and that you want to continue feeling free! Hold that thought, you've rid yourself of your own guilt, let's discuss how you contend with the onslaught of others' assumptions as well.

Chapter 5 - Assumptions of ME

Liberate yourself from assumptions

Andrea's story

I think the assumptions may be from our parents.

"I'm Andrea, I've been married for six years and have two boys under five. My husband has a good job, I just earn a bit more than him in my work as a consultant.

It's interesting to think about people's assumptions regarding the woman as ME. My friends don't bat an eyelid at it because a lot of the females in my group who I've grown up with are also in a similar situation. I think where I do possibly get more frustrated is with Ralph's friends, because the men seem to assume things, they seem to think like it's an alpha-male type situation and that if they're going out to work, the women will just stay at home. They have much more traditional views of male and female which I don't come across in my group.

We found that when we moved out of London after my first child and we moved to the suburbs it was very different to London. Where we lived, generally the men went out and had very good jobs and brought back the money and there were lots of housewives who looked brilliant, immaculate and looked after the kids and had a huge fantastic car and that type of thing, and I found I was definitely the only woman who worked or had anywhere near an equal salary to their husband and it was alien to them, absolutely alien. Whereas when we moved back into London, it's just the norm.

My friends are quite a female group who I've known since childhood, many who have moved down to London. His group met at university. My frame of reference is the group that I'm in. In the mothers' group, there were lots who seemed to be lawyers, solicitors, very professional women in this area. So the assumptions are a lot freer in this group. There will be assumptions, but I don't find so many in relation to being ME.

I think the assumptions may be from our parents. His mum worked actually, she was quite unusual in that she wasn't home very much. It was his grandmother who looked after him. I know when I did have children I do remember my Mum saying to me: "Well I stayed at home with you until you were four, I hope you're going to do the same," and I said: "No, probably not."

Maybe it's just in the male group that they haven't quite caught up with how many females are thinking. For women it's maybe been more of an issue. I think until it's forced, they don't need to think about it so much.

I've had to bite my tongue for the sake of his friendships and not saying to his friends, 'that's a ridiculous view'. I have also felt that I have to explain my situation in the mothers' group as it might seem strange that I like work so much. I explained the reason I work so much is that if we didn't, that would be quite a change to our lifestyle.

If Ralph was at home, although he still earns a very good salary, there would be visible signs that he was not ME, his friends' assumptions would then be challenged as they don't expect that the man would be the one at home looking after the children.

In fact when we talked about him being a stay-at-home dad, he said he'd be absolutely fine with it. The only area that would kind of niggle is what his friends would say. His friends would probably take the mickey".

Assumptions are rife in your life, you use them to make sense of your experience. So much information comes your way that you need to put things and people in categories so you don't get overloaded. Although these categories have their uses in terms of making sense of the world and making decisions, they can also be constraining for you, leading to stereotyping, bias and assumptions. You are not the only one, we all do it. As ME you will not fit into a typical category, those around you may find that confusing and therefore challenging. This results in assumptions made by them which are not always helpful.

Justify ME

One of the biggest issues that you will have as ME is other people's ideas of how you should be living your life. Don't feel that you have to justify or explain yourself, however, sharing can help. Andrea is lucky in that she has a group of supportive friends who identify with her situation. Your support network can be the difference between coping and crashing out of the ME role. Andrea raises a good question: Are men being left behind with their views? The answer is probably that it depends on your social circle, geographical location, cultural background and the situation. Waiting staff in restaurants always give my husband the bill, tradespeople always want to speak to the man of the house. How do you challenge these assumptions without causing embarrassment or seeming to be boosting your own ego? Your emotional intelligence and consideration for others mean that you often shy away from challenging others' wrongly held beliefs about roles in the family unit.

How interesting that the women Andrea met in the suburbs frowned at her career-woman status when she was located there. Assumptions come from all directions: parents; new and existing groups of friends; colleagues; and don't forget ourselves. Are you where you thought you would be at twenty, thirty, forty, fifty, sixty years old? What happens when the expectation doesn't meet the reality? How do we let go of the assumptions we had about what we should be doing? Some views are firmly set in the past and don't equate with your current reality.

It's easier to shrug off some assumptions more easily than others, particularly if the person sharing their assumptions is someone you respect and admire. How much significance should you give to others' voices? Take some time to consider what their underlying assumptions are. Andrea's example of her mother suggesting that she stay at home until her children are four years-old is a familiar one. When someone close to you overlays their experience it is often hard to break free from it, especially when they gave birth to you! It was right for them but it might not be right for you.

There are many ways to handle it:

Discuss the differences and similarities between their situation and yours.

Subtly provide them with examples of others who have also done what you are doing so that they can see it can work.

Just do what you are doing confidently and well - they will come round.

Then there's the justification for why you ended up taking the route you did. Like Andrea said, she felt the need to justify why she loved working by explaining the consequences of her not doing so to the mothers' group. In many ways, the only justification should be to yourself and those who really matter. As soon as you are justifying yourself you are putting yourself in a defensive position, which can be seen by others as an excuse. Your rationale is firmly rooted in your current life situation which won't be clear to others outside of it. I don't hear stay-at-home mums justifying themselves, do you?

Often those who are not sure about the route they are taking will be the most challenging to you, they are not really questioning you, they are challenging themselves. When they ask: 'How do you manage? I couldn't do that,' sometimes what they're saying is: 'Could I try to do that?' or: 'Actually, if I did I might fail,' so they stay doing what they are doing. Others are just curious about how you make your corner of the world work, if it's genuine, share your experience to help a fellow potential ME.

Partners can also be put in a difficult position by others' assumptions: Victoria recalls a recent holiday where a fellow male traveller said to her husband: "She books the holidays and you pay, isn't that the way it goes?" when it definitely wasn't. The traveller was met with a stony silence, which he probably struggled to interpret as it didn't fit with the framing of how he saw the world. How should her husband have handled that? Should he have said, "well actually my wife paid and she is the main earner," or agreed with the traveller, even though it wasn't true? It's a difficult one. We are thrust into situations every day where we can fit in or stand out, with the easy option there will also be some tension. Revisit the values that you noted down in Chapter 1, what do they tell you is the right approach? Combine this with the various worlds you inhabit and decide on the appropriate approaches for each situation.

How you handle it is up to you, ultimately it's your business and although sharing will reduce stigma in the long term, you need to share when and if you become ready. Every time you step out in the world as ME, you make it better and easier for the next person.

The ideal state is one where you have enough internal confidence to not be concerned about others' influences. This can take time as initially, you will build a barrier to protect yourself. Seek out others who can reinforce your way of being, so that your confidence and peace of mind radiates warmth, rather than feeling attacked by others.

The right decisions for you

Remember how this decision for you to become ME came about, whether it was a choice you made or the world made for you, you made a considered decision to make the most of your circumstances. Sometimes you are going towards something, looking at your long term future - financial security, lifestyle and independence, other times being ME enables you to maintain the status quo and stop major unsettling changes happening in your family's life, like changing school, moving home, downsizing. Keep yourself anchored, recognising that the route you choose was the best way forward. This forms an umbrella, protecting you from the acid rain of others' assumptions rather than letting them saturate you.

Embarrassed ME

Embarrassed that your partner is earning less than you? This isn't the way it's meant to be!

The truth is, you grew up thinking things would be different, it may not have been that a member of royalty would sweep you off your feet, but it probably wasn't, 'I am going to be in a relationship, have children and be ME.' Your modern day fairy tale is different to the ones in the books, but nevertheless can have an equally happy ending. In her talk on vulnerability, Brene Brown speaks about vulnerability being central to who we are and being neither good nor bad, but necessary. Instead of feeling vulnerable, experiencing shame and fear as ME, we should 'practice gratitude' and 'lean into joy', and believe that 'we are enough.'

Families come in many shapes and forms now, what would it take to shift that shame to pride?

Would you feel more pride if you were both not working and had to make other, less palatable changes in your life?

REFLECTION

Revisit your reflections in your journal from Chapter 2 on Choice - review all the choices available to you, the skills, qualities and attributes that enable you to make good choices. Use these to remind yourself that you are making the right decisions for your family.

What anchors you to the decision you are making? Is it your values, or would you define it differently? Capture it on a small piece of paper or post-it note, in a word or a quick line drawing and keep it in your purse. Open it up whenever you are feeling unsure to remind you of the good anchored and grounded decisions that you are making and to protect you from others' assumptions.

Who is benefitting and how?

Because you can't and choose not to do it *all* any longer, you will be empowering those around you through trust and delegation. You will be role-modelling a way of being ME. Knowing this should create a warm glow inside you, radiating outwards to combat the assumptions about what is right for you. This internal knowing, combined with your values and the pioneering word you chose in Chapter 1, will root you firmly so that the blowing winds of assumptions will not knock you over.

You are teaching children how to be in the world, not just in the home. Sally says, "I think what I see my role being is perhaps as someone who can actually guide people into the world because it's quite a difficult world to come into for them and they do come to me for that sort of advice and guidance. You know, how do you, or how would you, or what about this. That's a real positive, that I've got that ability to do that."

You are utilising the skills of those around you rather than dumping and criticising, you are valuing and helping those that matter to you to grow and develop, so they too can go out into the world confidently.

Through speaking to MEs, I have been heartened by the success stories of women making their corner of the world work. Their partners have been happy in their roles and their children have benefitted from typically spending more time with their other parent than they would have traditionally.

Your happiness can resonate from many places:

* Knowing that you are making a significant impact at work

* Knowing that you are fulfilled by your work
* Knowing that your family is well cared for
* Knowing that you have financial security and can maintain your lifestyle
* Sharing your hopes and dreams
* Knowing that you have a degree of independence
* Knowing that the balance of family, work and relationships is right for you
* Knowing the risk you take is calculated and designed to enhance your future

It's OK to be different

There are so many instances in history where people who have thought or acted differently, have opted out of fitting in and created their own groups. Think of Al Gore's stand on climate change and Lady Gaga's extravagant stage wear. Arianna Huffington, founder of the Huffington Post, has nap rooms in her company. Amongst other very different approaches to work, she knows that the best ideas often come when you wake up from a nap and she has decided to integrate the opportunity for sleep into the working day. What's stopping you?

Step out and be courageous, in many ways you are already doing it, just take one small step at a time.

Rhonda is creating an internal group at work as she is one of the few senior women in the organisation to have a baby, she wants to pave the way for others but also help the organisation understand the needs of women who are MEs.

How you create a group is up to you, but here are some ideas to stimulate your thinking:

Surfing the net - online - you can create groups on most social media sites

Many networks exist around good food, start a breakfast, lunch, dinner or just a coffee club

There are many business and professional networking groups in existence; you could approach them to form a special interest group for MEs

Your group, although consisting of MEs, doesn't have to be focused on that, maybe you could start a book club, exercise group, drawing group, or a speech-making group, just so that you can come together. You will find more ideas on how to do this in Chapter 12.

Women as hunter gatherers

Being ME is the most natural thing in the world, because women's prime concern has always been to look after the family. Your primitive animal instinct kicks in to nurture and protect. With your increasing income earning potential, it makes sense that you now have an equal choice about whether you choose to work, and if you can provide the best for your family.

As I mentioned in the Introduction to this book, women being ME is new to Western society, but not so new in other parts of the world. Women were, and still are in some African tribes, accepted hunter gatherers. They would go out and hunt the dinner while the men tended to the chores at home. Lucky for us we can just pop to the supermarket.

I am not sure if you have chosen the partner who fits in with who you are, or whether you have adapted to fit with them, but you will complement each other and become both halves of the whole. What's clear is that one person's career becomes the priority and that is the ME, the other then has to take a back seat and needs to be more flexible in order to enable the ME to flourish.

Have you had this conversation - where is the flexibility in your relationship?

Trendsetter

Whether you like it or not you now wear the badge of trendsetter or pioneer.

Your challenge is to let go of your assumptions and those of others about who you should be. Instead, decide who you want to be and create that unique vision of you. I have carefully constructed a guided visualisation podcast to help you do just that, you can listen to it at www.rockingyourrole.com

REFLECTION

* What is right about your path?
* What does it give you?
* Who must you value?
* How should you value them?
* What must you do?

The intense peer pressure that you may experience as ME is akin to that which you experienced in the playground - that need to fit in and not stand out. What would you advise someone who was experiencing that to do? Now take your own advice!

Here are some ways to snap out of those assumptions:

Hold the opposite view to those with the assumption.

Women are the best MEs because...

Check out if you would want to give up being ME, be the homemaker for the week. How does it fit?

Imagine the worst-case scenario of being ME - acknowledge and recognise why that's not you.

Chapter 6 - Stop ME

Know what you don't need to do

Sally's story

We've had extremely good weekends where I've just been able to focus on the family possibly better than if I spent more time with them feeling distracted. Yes, I think I'm finally learning that one.

"Hi my name is Sally. I'm in my early fifties, I have three children, two of whom have grown up and just about left home. I'm married; I live with my husband and I've been ME for the last twenty-two years. So we're quite the veterans of this, he does all the care responsibilities, the house-keeping responsibilities; I do the breadwinning side of it. I work as an Interim Manager so I'm away a lot, I tend to be home at the weekends. I found a job that suited me at a time when he found a job that didn't suit him, so we switched and just carried on that way and it seems to have worked.

I'm speaking to quite a lot of women now who are starting out on the ME route and when I say, actually I've been doing it for the last two decades, there is a sort of element of surprise. I have the benefit of financial independence and, because I've been out in the real world, I can relate to the children differently to how I would have done, perhaps, if I had been the one that was at home.

I feel quite good actually. I went for a run this morning in London and I was sort of thinking 'what are my next ambitions for the next ten years or so?' And I thought, yes I'm quite happy with the arrangement.

I've got memories of when the children were a lot younger of trying to write reports with a child sitting on my back and things like that, or of taking them swimming and then trying to do reading whilst sitting in the café, you know. So just trying to squeeze things in and sometimes even now when I'm at home, I feel guilty if I'm working because I think if I'm at home I should be with *you*, so I'm always still trying to squeeze work in. So at home, I appear as if all I'm doing is spending time with the kids.

At the moment, I'm having really very limited time at home and what works best is if I feel that I can just put work aside and concentrate on being there. We've had extremely good weekends where I've just been able to focus on the family, possibly better than if I spent more time with them feeling distracted. Yes. I think I'm finally learning that one."

William Bridges in his book, *Transitions*, says that all beginnings start with endings. You will need to stop doing some things in order to make space for your new behaviours to come through. This is a challenge, because I am sure that everything you are doing right now seems essential.

Remembering that your time is a precious commodity to be valued and used wisely can help you start to be ruthless about what you spend it on. You will start to switch off auto-pilot and begin to be more conscious of what you are doing and why. This increases awareness of your patterns of behaviour. Noticing the small things that can make a big difference will give you the impetus to stop doing the things you don't need to do.

Don't think of this as a New Year resolution like losing weight or getting fit, instead make it as small and natural as brushing your teeth in the morning and it should only take a few minutes a day. Any change should be just like that.

Time is precious

Sorry to be morbid, but imagine that this was your last day on earth. When you look back, how much time did you waste? What constitutes waste is things that serve no-one; watching your favourite TV show with a mug of hot chocolate might be a relaxing wind down after a long day for you, but sitting planted in front of the TV for six hours with a bottle of wine probably won't make you feel good.

I used to have to drive a lot for work. I found listening to music on the radio mind-numbingly boring, as I felt it was repetitive. I started to invest in audio books, I was listening to stories and my journey flew by, the time was no longer wasted. If you constantly treat time as a precious commodity, you won't fritter it away.

Be present when you're there

I know you've done it - been cooking a meal, helping your child with homework and been on the phone to a friend who needs support at the same time. You feel proud of your multi-tasking skills but is anyone really getting what they need from the mediocre-quality time?

Very much like the workplace, the hours you spend don't necessarily equate to the quality of output. Presenteeism exists in the home as well as the workplace, the need to be seen even if you are not contributing physically or mentally. I am not saying don't go home, it's just that the Quality Vs Quantity rule definitely applies here.

I know from my coaching work that focused attention is a gift that we all value, when was the last time you gave it? This perspective on your time, could also help you, is one date night with your partner compensation for not really giving them much attention all week? Or would five minutes of real attention every day be much better? You will have to experiment with this for yourself and find out what works. One thing's for sure, you can save yourself hours of non-quality time, when you are physically there but your mind is elsewhere and everyone knows it.

You may think that your time is the only time that counts, but actually quality time from others can be just as valuable to those around you. You may have friends or family members with more time on their hands who would be happy to help out an elderly relative, or you may know people who have children the same age as yours who would welcome a playdate. This takes the pressure off as they get quality attention from others. You will still need and will want to provide it, but knowing that it is also coming from elsewhere will ease the strain.

Superwoman syndrome

I see women falling foul of the syndrome on a daily basis, dropping like flies as they leave the train station: 'I might as well do it myself as no one can do it as well as me,' 'I have a handle on it all,' 'If I have to stay up until midnight catching up on my work so that I can attend musical theatre practice or football practice, it's worth it,' are their familiar mantras.

Listen and listen carefully, *it's OK not to be able to do it all.*

Repeat after me, *it's OK not to be able to do it all.*

Now say it out loud, *it's OK not to do be able to do it all.*

Our ability to *'do it all'* is a consistent theme from every woman I have spoken to, but a myth I think we perpetuate - just like the one that supermodels don't have cellulite... Right!

Alicia describes how we are victims of our own ability, we just get up and do, unable to say no:

"I'm a private pilot and it's mostly men in my small little flight club. The women just get up and do. Now it's got to the point that they're afraid to do anything without sending me an email asking me: 'What do you think about this Alicia?' and I think: 'Oh no, I created a monster!' A lot of times I'll tease them, I'll say: 'Why don't you go and ask your wife, she's been doing things for a very long time you know, because you just can't make that decision yourself' and they just crack up because I know a lot of their spouses. It's so funny, I just have to shake my head a lot, these guys cannot make a decision."

Your capability can render others incapable, be careful not to overplay your strength and leave those around you too weak to contribute.

It's OK not to

Working gives you fulfilment; it's a place where you can just be you, rather than another of your familiar roles. It's a space for your ambition and development, where success and accomplishment can be more easily measured. Sometimes it's a place where your decisions can make the world a better place. You know, I admit it, I would rather spend a day doing my book-keeping, the job I most procrastinate over, rather than attending a school trip. I love my child but I am not sure if I want to spend a day with twenty-nine children who belong to other people. It's OK not to want or need to attend every school trip or community function. You can compensate for it by having a weekend of fun or having quality time on family holidays, doing things you *like* doing together. However, watch out for warning signs, if your family stop including you in their plans, your relationship is on the rocks or you just don't want to go home, you may be loving your work that bit too much.

ME, stay-at-home mum

It's OK not to want to be a stay-at-home mum. Although the idea sometimes sounds attractive, Andrea knows being a stay-at-home mum is not right for her: "What if I weren't the breadwinner anymore? If things changed I'd be quite happy to earn the same as Ralph, but having had a position of breadwinner, maybe it makes money more important. I wouldn't say I'm a financially driven person, but it does give you something to put you on that equal footing and if you took it away, that would be strange."

When are you at your best? In flow, relaxed, confident and comfortable, at your happiest? Share this information with those who matter, help them understand how your happiness at work increases happiness at home. What happens when you don't do these things? What's good enough? How can you experiment?

Perfectly imperfect ME

It's OK not to have a roast dinner on the table each night and the perfect home.

There will be unintended consequences of your need to try to do everything. Your high standards will be standards that everyone will have to achieve and if you aren't achieving them yourself, how can others? The result is that everyone is left feeling that they are not good enough, ultimately resulting in them not trying, or feeling resentful. The impact is that you end up doing even more.

Explain why you love your work and how it enhances your life and that of the family. Victoria recalls returning to work after maternity leave and how she cherished being herself again. She was delighted to be seen as an individual rather than in the role of mother.

You may be familiar with the work of Eric Berne, a psychoanalyst who created a theory of communication called *Transactional Analysis*. His theory was built upon by Taibi Kahler (1975) who developed *Driver Behaviour*. *Driver Behaviour* is unconscious and a place we often go to under stress, it is two-way in that you expect it of yourself AND others. The drivers he defines are: Be Perfect, Be Strong, Try Hard, Please Others, Hurry Up, one or two of these may spring off the page at you immediately as driving your behaviour.

You can find out more about them by going to www. rockingyourrole.com for more details.

REFLECTION

Knowing your drivers can help you work to the best of them rather than be driven by them.

How could your drivers impact the way you feel about, and are undertaking, your role as ME?

Yes, Mrs Invincible, it's OK to get help even if no one you know or anyone in your family ever had a cleaner, gardener or ironing service, you can be the first and you know what? What you start they'll follow! You don't have to do it all, manage it all and make all the decisions. Get practical support and other forms of help if you need it, such as coaching, counselling, therapy, colleagues and critical friends. Connie said that contracting services like gardening was one of the best things she ever did and lists it as one of the three most important lessons she learnt as ME.

Even if you don't know if the service exists, start thinking about it. If you enjoy it and it's not taking up valuable quality time with those who matter, then don't contract it out. But otherwise, why not? Be honest, you can't do it all and why should you!

Think about how much you earn an hour. I'll bet that these services cost considerably less and you're likely to help another woman ME just like you in the process.

ACTION - What can you contract out?

Look at the list below, what would be helpful to contract out? How will you find out more about doing this? When will you have done it by? What would be the benefit?

Ironing

Washing

Cooking

Cleaning

School run

Gardening

Decorating

Tutoring

Dog walking

Hairdressing

Add your own

Commit to when you will source the service, trial it for at least a month and review how it's working for you.

You're wonderful, but...

You're wonderful, but not invincible. Like everything in this book, it starts with you. You are likely to be a giving person and maybe feel that you give more to others than yourself. In reality you are not capable of giving to others unless you give to yourself. So actually the first gift of quality time should be to you. It can be as short as fifteen minutes of precious attention, listening to yourself while relaxing in the bath, to a full-on weekend retreat.

 REFLECTION

When was the last time you had quality time and how did you feel?

What was different and how can you recreate it?

Tips for valuing your precious time:

* Be present when you're there!

* Be ruthless - block time out, even if it's just fifteen minutes, better than an hour of mediocre quality time.

* Don't overdo it, don't save a week's worth of nagging to be distilled into 30 minutes of so-called quality time.

* Don't sacrifice yourself for the sake of quality time. Planning to work after children are asleep and you've had two hours quality time with your partner is occasionally OK, it's still putting yourself last.

* Time expands for a while, but not for long, like an elastic band it will pop back and sting you or break. Don't abuse your body and mind.

* Pay attention to your body, it will give you messages if something's not right.

Switch off auto-pilot

Switch off auto-pilot and take the controls for a while. The truth must be told, however harsh it may be; it may redden your eyes, but it won't blind you.

ALMADOU KOUROUMA

My husband asked my daughter how she was the other day. She immediately said she was fine. She'd had a bad day at school and had told me all about it, so I reminded her that she wasn't fine, she responded: "That's my usual answer." Often the truth is that we are not fine. We all think we are being truthful with ourselves and others, until we really sit down and question, how am I, really?

Notice how long ago you may have learnt your standard answer, you may not have been truthful for some time now.

When you reveal how you are really feeling, you may realise that trying to be all things to all people is not working for you: that you really like working but can't admit it to others; that actually you are a bit embarrassed about earning more than your partner; and that you're mourning a loss of femininity as a result of being what you see as being both the man and woman of the house. I have concentrated on these, but you may also realise some other feelings, work with them, there will be solutions if you focus.

Have you ever put something away safely and then had no recollection of where you put it? Found your way to work with no real recollection of the journey? Had a conversation with someone and can't remember what you spoke about? You were probably on auto-pilot, going through the motions of your life that you have done so often, without being conscious of what you were doing. A part of your mind that has done it so many times before takes over and you are a bit like an electrical appliance in sleep mode.

Although this mode is getting you through life - you eventually find what you've put away, you are getting to work, and engaging with people - but you don't know if things could be better, you don't know what you are missing, because you are not aware of it. You could have better conversations, journeys and storage space or you may not need to be travelling, conversing or storing stuff at all. You are living the unquestioned life. Think more:

Some activities like ironing socks I would find a complete waste of time, others might find it therapeutic - if you have a choice between ironing and delivering on your report deadline, which do you drop?

Nagging, arguing, moaning - what else could you be focusing on. What are the positives?

You may be acting out an ideal image, illusion, or someone else's vision of who you should be and what you should be doing.

Where did you learn to be like this, nurture or nature? Is what your experience tells you right?

ACTION - 1 Week of Questioning

Spend 1 week being ruthlessly critical of your use of time, every day look at your diary and challenge what's in there. Engage the curiosity of a child and ask yourself naïve questions. Here are some questions for you, but I am sure you'll have more.

* Why do I drive, could I get the train?
* Why am I attending that meeting?
* Why do I spend 40 minutes on the phone when I could be doing something better?
* Who will read the report I've just written, should I have just picked up the phone?
* How productive was my day?
* What am I doing that's just plain crazy?
* What am I *not* doing that seems like basic common sense?
* Hold the questions that you can't answer and the answers that you don't believe.

When the week is up, choose one thing to change for the next week and review it, continue to keep tweaking how you use your time to make the best of it.

Big things don't matter

Big things don't matter, small things do. Some activities are a complete waste of time. When I have a really early start for work, say I need to catch a 6am flight, I find I wake up on numerous occasions during the night worrying that I've missed the alarm. Ridiculous isn't it! You can spend your time worrying about things when there is already an early warning alarm in place, it's the other stuff that you need to think about. For example, if you don't pay your rent or mortgage, do your job well, or send your child to school, someone will let you know straightaway that things need to change. Birth and death are taken care of by the universe, but who reminds you about the small stuff? The small things mount up and can become huge. Just like those lovely displays of tins in the supermarket, they can come toppling down and cause a lot of destruction.

Are you wondering what the small things are? The things that make life worth living, like your humanity, warmth, kindness, opportunities to laugh together, the family sitting round the dinner table and, dare I say it ... love.

Small things bring joy

Victoria described just bringing home a selection of herbal teas for her partner who really appreciated the fact that she had thought of him.

Random acts of present-ness, such as finishing work early once in a while, a surprise collection from nursery or school (if it's not too un-cool to do so) can bring joy to those you care about. This approach of spontaneity and surprise means that no one is let down, you are under-promising and over-delivering, which is always the best way. You are finding ways to do what you want to do and please others in the process without feeling committed.

Make dates

Explain what you are capable of and willing to offer. Victoria's daughter would love her to be a dinnerlady, she likes the idea of seeing her Mum at lunchtime each day. One day, Victoria had to sit her daughter down and explain that she loves her work and that it made her who she is and that being a dinnerlady, whilst it would be great to see her daughter every day, was not going to make her a happy Mummy. Her daughter accepted it and understood. Instead of feeling guilty, Victoria moved to a place of helping her child understand that work can be a part of you and a pleasurable one, a much more valuable lesson.

Understand what those closest to you really want, rather than what you think they need. Your perception of what your family wants and what it actually needs may be different. Sondra thought that, when her PhD study ended after five years of not being around and maintaining a full-time job, that her girls would be delighted. Instead, they had to adjust to the intense interest of their mother, which they had escaped. I am not saying that this was a bad thing, but the opportunity for greater independence - while initially rejected - is not one that can be given up easily.

 ACTION - stop look listen

List - what are you going to stop doing today e.g. relinquishing the burden of responsibility.

Take the weight off. Commit to your ME **don't** do list today.

Chapter 7 - Communicating ME

Communication is critical

Spoken words are living things like cocoa-beans packed with life. And like cocoa-beans they grow and give life... They will enter some insides, remain there and grow like the corn blooming on the alluvial soil at the river side.

GABRIEL OKARA

Communication is at the centre of making your world work and is critical for healthy ME relationships. What form does your communication take? Are you aware of the power of your communication?

Communication is two-way - you also need to listen. The strange thing is that even though you are supporting your family, you can sometimes act as through you are completely on your own. When you do this you close people out and don't feel the need to communicate. This is a big mistake and one that you need to correct immediately.

Two-way communication with those that are important to you are critical to making your role work and by two-way, communication, I don't mean just waiting your turn to speak, I mean really listening to what others have to say too.

The more you talk about being ME, the more it will become the norm, so work on finding ways and avenues to speak about it. The more you do it, the easier it will become.

How you feel about being ME can change regularly, you need to have regular discussions as the situation changes, to notice the ebb and flow of these changes and how dramatic they are.

You cannot communicate enough, it is the key to making things work. Do it, set aside time, and ensure it's not just you.

ME ego

Fallen into the trap of believing in your own self importance? This financial independence, often in a senior position, doesn't make you a more important person. Keep that ego in check, even if at work they adore you and no one dares to question you. In my experience of coaching senior leaders, their work lives are often lacking honest feedback, however much they ask for it. Staff around them are nervous of saying what they think due to the imbalance of power inherent in the relationship and so they exist in a bubble, where they think everything they do is right and they are always agreed with. It can be an extremely lonely place, which is why they come for coaching.

The combination of the senior role at work and ME role at home can become a heady cocktail that can make you think that you are the only one who has something valid to say. Seek out and listen to the feedback and don't become full of hubris.

Victoria describes the money and power taking over and how she practically redecorated her home around her husband without asking for his input. When he questioned how much she had spent on new items, she recalls saying: "It's my money, I'll do what I want with it." She now realises that this wasn't the right way to go about things and why that led to a number of heated arguments. She realises the importance of communication now and that the message she was giving was: 'My opinion is the only one that matters as I am holding the purse strings.' Luckily her relationship survived, many relationships wouldn't. She believes it was largely down to talking about it.

This may seem unnecessary to you because I am sure that you consider yourself to be very sensitive to the needs of those that matter to you, but spend a few minutes reflecting on the following questions just to be sure.

REFLECTION

How much are you discussing big decisions - or is it all your way?

When was the last time you discussed where you are taking your career and what that means for those around you?

What makes it feel like you are holding the purse strings? Is that right for your relationship?

Ideas spring from communication

One of the wonderful benefits of investing your valuable time and energy in communicating, is that ideas and new perspectives spring from it. When you are mentally and physically exhausted and have been juggling roles all day, you may not be the best person to make decisions or see things from different viewpoints. Talking things through can really help and you will benefit from someone else's energy to transport you along for a change. Instead of walking up that escalator because you know it's good for the thighs and you think you'll get there faster, you can stand still and let it take you to where you need to go.

Victoria recalls having a chat with a female colleague twenty years older than her one day when she was feeling particularly downtrodden, "I was moaning about my partner and how I was working so hard and how he would happily stay at home if I let him and Lavinia gently reminded me that he was enabling me to pursue my career, and that I couldn't do half the things I did if he didn't take up the slack. Although I didn't acknowledge what she said at the time, I reflected on it and thought, yes she's right. If I had a really driven and ambitious husband I would need to take on a different role or get a live in nanny which wouldn't have suited me."

Talking about it helped to shift Victoria's perspective on her role as ME. If she had kept the problem to herself, seething away under the surface, it would have got bigger. Lavinia had experienced a different life to Victoria. She had been married young and was a stay-at-home mum for most of her life, but still had wise words to offer, so don't dismiss those whom you assume won't understand.

Wise words of wisdom can come from the most unusual places.

 REFLECTION

If you are feeling that you are too exhausted or have exhausted your ideas on how to make things work for you as ME, who could you turn to for an idea-generating conversation?

Who haven't you spoken to yet about this specific issue who always offers you good advice?

What type of professional might you engage to support you? Perhaps your work would invest in a professional coach or mentor for you?

Have you really spoken to your partner and clearly asked for what you need? If not, try the activity on the next page.

ACTION - Asking for support

This is a way in which you can frame your request for support from your partner. I would recommend that you plan what you are going to say in advance and ask your partner to listen to you uninterrupted while you say it, then you can engage in conversation around it:

I see the current situation as being like this... (describe the situation in as much detail as possible)	e.g. I see the current situation as difficult because I am coming home exhausted and not having any family time
This makes me think... (talk about what you think)	e.g. this makes me think that things need to change as I am becoming distant from family life
This makes me feel... (talk about the emotion involved)	e.g. this makes me feel really upset, lonely and a bit alienated from my own family
What I need is... (describe in detail what you are looking for)	e.g. what I need is for us to find ways to change this so I do feel that I am part of the family and that this is a manageable situation

This way of planning works equally well in other situations where you need to give feedback. I share it with my coaching clients who need to give difficult feedback to staff and colleagues. It enables them to plan what they are going to say and become less caught up in their own emotions so that the message lands with who is receiving it first time. If you have something that you need to say, plan it now in your journal.

Listening is a gift

This process of two-way communication is not just to ensure that you are heard; really listening to someone is a gift and makes the other person feel valued. It always surprises me when I am delivering leadership training how many people really need to develop their listening skills. They speak over each other, do other things such as answering emails on their smart phone while others are talking to them and sometimes you can actually see a whole other conversation going on in their head. What does it mean to really listen? It means stop thinking about what you want to do next, stop adding to your to-do list, stop waiting for your turn to add something to the conversation that you think will enhance it, instead give your full attention to that person.

Do you remember the last time you were really listened to, what did the person do that helped you realise you were being listened to, what did you notice about them. How did it make you feel? Is there anything from this that you can emulate?

 ACTION - Improving communication

Three ways to improve your two-way communication.

Try really listening, just once a week. Focus, hear, give time to someone who deserves it and notice the shift in them.

Explain how you would like to be listened to. For example, you may just want to offload but your partner may want to solve your problem. Explain to them that you don't want solutions or digression, just good old-fashioned listening.

Put yourself in their shoes. Your partner may have been at home all day looking after the home and children, a role that is undervalued. Using your listening skills, value, appreciate, accept without criticism and notice the results.

Making ME the norm

To give up the task of reforming society is to give up one's responsibility as a free [wo]man.

ALAN PATON

Communication is important if you want to remove the stigma around your role as ME. Right now, you being ME isn't the norm; if it were, you wouldn't be reading this book. My hope is there will be much less stigma associated with it in the future. In order for this to happen, you need to talk about it. Talking about it doesn't just help to reduce the stigma but it can also increase the quality of support you'll receive. Think about plastic surgery, the more people were honest about their nips and tucks, the more it was recognised that it needed to be regulated. Now there is a plethora of support available to help you choose the right plastic surgery option for you. It's now OK to admit to having it, so it moved from being a taboo to being OK.

Sally, who has been ME for twenty-two years, describes her family moving from denial to acceptance of her as ME: "There was quite a while of pretending it wasn't really happening that way round, until it became inevitable. Family members would pretend it was only a temporary arrangement, or it was a bit sort of glossed over; the fact that we had reversed roles. It took them quite a long time to actually accept this is what it is."

Finding the words

One thing that struck me is the lack of vocabulary for the role of ME. When I speak to women they say: "I am in a role reversal relationship," or: "My husband stays at home, while I go out to work." They generally stumble over these descriptions, because there is no vocabulary available for their situation. The titles 'house husband' and 'female breadwinner' are borrowed from the other gender and don't sit quite right, we need to be more creative and realistic about what these roles are. When a man stays at home to look after the family or a woman becomes ME, you are not swapping like for like, the roles are performed differently, not better or worse, and the descriptions need to be different as a result. The absence of the vocabulary may mean that you can't have the conversations, and both parties struggle to articulate their role in the relationship. By communicating you help your partner who is earning less to be able to articulate their situation and so create a path for others to follow in the future.

In my work with senior leaders, I use a number of personality questionnaires based on the work of Carl Jung to help individuals and teams understand their preferences for kinds of communication, to enable them to improve, be more flexible and adapt their approach. They provide a framework in which to discuss how you communicate and why we don't appreciate each other sometimes. You may have undertaken something similar in your workplace. If so, dig it out, remind yourself of your preferences and consider the preferences of those you want to communicate with. If you haven't got a framework, it may be something you want to consider. There are many trained psychologists and coaches who can provide you with the personality questionnaire and most importantly, give you helpful feedback.

You may say, 'Well, the next generation will be OK.' I agree, they will be, but only if you pave the way. The suffragettes wouldn't have imagined the struggles women still have in the workplace, things have moved a long way, but some barriers still exist. I have spoken a lot about communication with your partner but communication with others is just as critical. In particular you have the opportunity to stop reinforcing the gender stereotypes to which they may be exposed from so many angles, including the media, school and the family.

REFLECTION

* When was the last time you discussed your roles in your relationship? Spend some time finding the words.

* How are you paving the way for others, even in a small way?

* How can you broach the subject of communication; would a personality questionnaire be a useful starting point?

Changeable ME

How you feel about being a ME can change regularly. How you feel about your role can be as changeable as the weather, because different things will affect it, some of which we touched on earlier in the book. If you haven't worked through these things, you will be like a feather blowing in the wind, rather than a tree rooted in the ground.

Communication is one of the few spaces for you to be vulnerable. Yes, I said the 'V' word. I know you go around being tough and giving everything to everyone, but there needs to be a space where you can air your fears, concerns and emotions, that feels safe. If you don't take this space, it will leak out elsewhere, like the coffee cup I mentioned in Chapter 1.

Underlying feelings of resentment and self sacrifice will eat away at you, so nip it in the bud. Talk about it. The communication can help you to rebalance the power in your relationships. It is particularly important for you when you hold the traditionally male role. You are demonstrating that your partner's thoughts and opinions are just as valid as yours. You are also demonstrating that you need support and help.

Things may need to change

Other times it could be that enough is enough, things need to change. The communication will help you notice if you are repeating yourself, daily, weekly, monthly, yearly or whether you may be repeating whole past relationships. These patterns of communication and relationships should be observed.

If you keep saying things in the same way and nothing is changing, do you need to change the way you communicate it?

Have you always been the ME in every relationship that you've had? Why is that?

REFLECTION

* What patterns are you repeating?

* What lessons can you learn?

* What are you doing over and over in the same way, expecting different results?

* What can you do differently?

Communication is critical because even the tiniest change could put everything else out of kilter. A complex network of reliance is what keeps the ME going, whether partner, childcare, grandparents etc. One down and it all goes into a spin. It is important that any changes are communicated on both sides. You can try to build in buffers for these such as giving yourself an extra hour in case there is traffic getting home, but there also needs to be communication.

Being ME may not be what you signed up for in a relationship, the deal may have been that you stay at home and your partner brings home the bacon. Making it clear that it needs to be temporary in that case is also important. Using this book will help you manage through it, and you may even change your view, but keep tabs on your health, wealth and emotional stability while you do, and keep communicating with your partner.

Daily changes

Daily events can change how you feel about being ME. As Andrea said, after she has had a holiday, it feels so much more difficult for her to go back to work knowing her husband and son will be at home together. This is one of her triggers or pressure points that she needs to be aware of. For you, it may be something else. Whatever it is, if you are aware you can manage it, you know it will pass, you can ask those closest to you to remind you.

Whatever your partner's role, it is likely to have its challenges also. If they are staying at home with children, these challenges are usually undervalued and, if they are also working, no matter how much they earn, work can be tough, remember to help your partner offload too.

What is your pattern for communication? How do you like to be communicated with in comparison to your partner? Is it different? When do you adapt, could you do it more often?

This activity will help you to understand your triggers, so you're prepared for the next time.

ACTION - Remind yourself

Think of the last time that you were temporarily dissatisfied with being ME.

Recall the time of year, where you were, who was present, what was going on in your life. How was your health, your wealth and emotions at the time?

What triggered it?

Was it something said, done, a situation?

How long did it last? Minutes, hours, days, months, or longer?

What did you do to overcome it? Actions, thoughts, talking, walking, breathing.

What can you learn from this to help it pass more quickly next time?

Use this information to help you the next time your ME buttons are pushed.

I hope that you've realised that you can't communicate too much. You as ME have much to gain from two-way communication. Work hard at carefully articulating your thoughts and feelings and help others to do the same. Most importantly... listen... not just with your ears but all of your heart and being ME will work for you.

Chapter 8 - Interdependent ME

Every action has a reaction

You are part of a system, every action has a reaction. You've probably grown up trying and striving to be responsible and independent, learning to survive and thrive on your own and I am sure that you encourage your children to do the same.

The reality is that you are kidding yourself if you really think you are independent as we are all *interdependent*. Your independence is an illusion, as it only exists within *inter*dependence.

We cannot exist without each other; everything we do impacts others and what they do impacts us. When I describe this idea to groups of leaders, I use a Hoberman Sphere like the image below. This very visual and interactive approach brings the concept to life. The sphere to the left is open and the one to the right is it in its collapsed form.

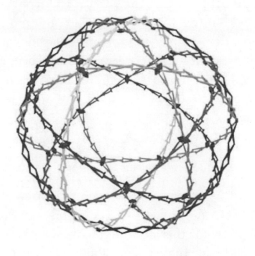

The sphere is made up of interconnected parts, patterns and shapes that all rely on each other to exist. I open and close the sphere to demonstrate how one small amount of pressure on only one part of the sphere can make the whole sphere collapse, while pulling at just one section on the collapsed sphere will make it enlarge and open up. Look at the image on the previous page. That sphere is your system and you are an integral part of it, you are essential to the whole. You will just be one small plastic length on your own, but together you are part of a beautifully interconnected system. When you look at the world from your point of view, it will differ from the whole picture, as you will only see one small part and not take into consideration all of the interdependencies, or the unforeseen consequences of your behaviour.

You are likely to have a preference for one perspective. As a woman, you may be more conditioned to consider all of the consequences within the system as a whole rather than thinking of yourself. You need to work on keeping both perspectives, and then multiple perspectives from different points in the system, in mind in order to make decisions which benefit both the whole and you as the individual within the system. This will come more naturally to some than others but is definitely a skill you can develop. Understanding that every action will have a reaction is central to this way of thinking; change doesn't exist in a vacuum.

Something as straightforward as deciding whether to apply for a promotion at work requires much more thought when you consider yourself within your system, as Rhonda illustrates:

"If we roll it back to three years ago before I was pregnant, then going for this job would have been a no-brainer. Now that I have these responsibilities, going for this job has been a real struggle because I really want it yet at the same time I know what I can get like. When I get a new position, the first nine months I really, really put my heart and soul into it to the detriment of other things, especially myself I would say, and that will have a big impact on my family life. I have decided to go for it because it will give us a bit more of a buffer zone financially than we have at the moment."

In this way, if Rhonda gets the promotion she has already discussed and explored as much as possible the consequences of her actions and the fact that the first nine months might be tough for them, while putting a timescale on it helps them to know there is light at the end of the tunnel. The family can then put things in place to get them through this period. Maybe they can book a holiday for ten months' time, or keep the children occupied so it won't feel like she is having to say no when they ask her to participate in activities. Or it could just be sitting down with the family and explaining the situation to everyone so that they are aware. Do you see the difference? As an individual, Rhonda likes to develop and take on new challenges, so from that perspective she was bound to go for the promotion, but she also took a step back and considered the system and all the interdependencies that allowed her to be ME.

Thriving

Know what your system needs to thrive. If your system is starved, it will diminish. You need to feed it - just like you would a plant, only nourishing it not with water, but whatever it needs. This could be: time together; caring words; quality attention; intimacy; appreciation. Have you taken the time to understand what the individuals within your system need from their point of view?

Often we think that what we need is what others do too, the saying, 'treat others as you would like to be treated' isn't true, rather it's, 'treat others as they would like to be treated.'

You can spend a lot of time trying to please others only to feel unappreciated and resentful. If this is happening to you then you are probably giving people what you think they want rather than what they actually do. Once in the dark days of boredom, when I was on maternity leave, I remember purchasing dividers for my husband's sock drawer and sorting it all out for him. A week later the drawer was back to its usual chaos and I was angry about the time I had spent on a job for him which he hadn't asked for or wanted. If I was going to do something special for him, he would rather that I watched sports with him once in a while as a gesture, even though it's not my thing. Yet actually it works for me, because I can do the shopping on the iPad at the same time! The same with my daughter. Yes, she wants Mum-ME daughter time, but she'll drop me in a heartbeat for someone her own age to play with; she doesn't actually need or want as much of my time as I think.

You are better off giving those in your system what they actually want - that is what will help your system thrive.

 ## ACTION - Observing

Start to be a bit more observant, stop being blinkered by what you think will make those around you happy and notice what actually does. You may find it makes your life a lot easier.

Consequences

Be mindful of changes that you make, they can have unforeseen consequences. Your position as ME means that you can sometimes believe that the world revolves around you. You are at the centre of your system and are vital to keeping it alive, and others need to react and deal with the impact of your actions because your role is so important. This attitude doesn't take into account or value what is keeping your system alive - the complex network of interdependencies that allow you to carry out your role.

Andrea has been married for six years, she has two children under five years old and runs her own consultancy business. She is ME, although her husband works full time and earns a good wage too, she just earns more. She says: "You're part of a system and that's going to shape how you fit into that system and the pieces you have around you. I've got a brilliant husband and I've got parents who gave me really great foundations and I've ended up the product of that, but it's always going to have to be sitting within the system."

To be comfortable with your system, you need to understand it now and in the potential long-term. Victoria has a passion for learning and when she studied three years ago, it meant she was away for four days at a time, which put strain on her husband. She was able to think about the benefit to the system long-term: increased earning potential, her happiness and also, role-modelling of continuous development for her daughter. She put things in place to ensure that her system could cope with the strain, such as additional support for school runs, sitting down with her daughter to explain why she was doing it, and it worked out for her. Without the attention to the system, issues could occur, and she may have had to drop out of her study.

Engage in understanding your system in order to make it work.

ACTION - map your relationships

Use the key below to map out your relationships with those in your system on a blank page in your journal. There is an example from Olive on the next page.

You will see she has strong relationships with her Mum and her husband, Ryan; has a distant relationship with her Dad and has some conflict with her son, Jack. By mapping her relationships in this way, it stood out to her that her husband Ryan had taken the role of the fun parent and she must seem like the authoritarian. She decided that she wanted to change this and that this was the area most important for her to focus on. She saw herself as the propeller on the front of a plane that needs to keep on turning to keep the plane flying. She said that she would never have viewed it this way without the mapping exercise and holds the image in her head.

Key

‑◻◻◻◻◻‑	strong and solid 2 way relationship	------------ distant relationship
>>>>>>>>>>	close relationship in which you dominate	———— simple working relationship
<<<<<<<<<<	close relationship in which the other partner dominates	≡≡≡≡ supportive relationship
‿‿‿	fun relationships	⬭ strong groups
××××××	conflictual relationships	⬭ weak groups
———//—	relationship that has been cut off	

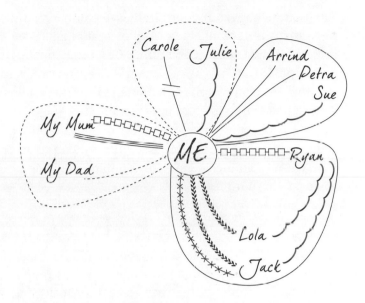

Use the key and a blank page in your journal and have a go at creating your own.

REFLECTION

❋ What is happening to the individuals within your system?

❋ What is happening in the spaces between the individuals?

❋ If your system was a piece of music, a meal, a place in the world, what would it be?

❋ What does this picture tell you about your system, points of strength, areas for development, what you need to focus on?

❋ What is your system wanting / needing / aspiring to achieve that is currently beyond its reach?

❋ Where do you need to start in order to make change occur in each of these relationships?

❋ To make change wider than the system you have drawn, what needs to shift in the system?

We focused above on your family system, but you will have many interconnected and overlapping systems, such as family, work, community or professional, and these could overlap. If you have friends at work or are self-employed and work from home, it is likely that your work and family systems may overlap. You may see it all as one big picture as, for you, work and family life could all be merged, or perhaps you see them as many different interconnected systems. It all depends on how you arrange your life.

It can be overwhelming to consider all of your systems at once because of the complex web of connections, and that is why I requested that you just start with your family system. However, you might want to map out others. This can be particularly useful to consider how the relationships within the work system are mapped and whether there is any change you need to make there. I also use this approach with senior leaders who want to consider where they needed to focus their attention within their teams to increase performance. You can also reflect on the overlap between the systems and how they are working for you. You might need to distance them or bring them closer together.

ME system - health

Constant awareness and flexibility will keep your system healthy. In your pursuit of keeping everything under control and keeping all the plates spinning, I can understand why you wouldn't seek out change, but the versatility and flexibility of you and your system are what will keep it working. Things will change for individuals within your system and for yourself and that ability to shift to accommodate it rather than crumble is important. Rather than being like the dry twigs that can snap easily, you need to be like the lithe green shoots that can bend and sway and be weaved into something else if necessary - malleable, fresh and alive.

Constant tweaking and understanding that things change but it will still be OK is crucial. This adaptability and versatility is important inside and outside of work and is also where you can fall down, especially when you are looking for balance. Balance within your system is the constant re-calibrating of priorities and interdependencies. It does not mean work time versus home time, but rather ensuring that no area is pushed too far so that it breaks and that all parts of the system are kept nourished. If you have a work project that needs your all for two weeks, you might not be able to do your once-a-week school run, so you could be concerned about the time you are not giving to your child. Instead consider what that time provides, perhaps it's insights into your child's day that they want to share with you? Communicate what is happening within your system, what will be different but also how you will capture those insights into your child's day at a different time instead of during the school run. The system is still nourished and it's adapting to the change. You may do this naturally, and if you do so, now you will do it more consciously and systematically.

 ACTION - System monitoring

* Gauge this once a week. How is our system doing; is this a blip, do I need to take action?

* Create changes to keep things flexible: the more routine, the harder things are to change, what can you tweak?

* Get ideas for doing things differently and be open to it - small changes, like having a cleaner could change your life. How can you remain aware of this?

Nourishing your system

What message did you receive about your family system when you were growing up? For some, it was to keep family matters private at all costs and for others, it was to be open and share with all. Whatever those messages were, you are likely to be considering them in your daily life even if it is to ensure that you do the opposite of what your upbringing taught you! Your illusion of independence can also be an overplayed strength, when you believe that it should mean that you don't need help, support and relationships with those outside your system as it would signify dependence.

Those women who are making it work are definitely opening up their system in order to give and gain support, share their experience and be the best they can be to make their corner of the world work. Whether it's Connie, who had a neighbour who supported her with childcare, or Femi, who has spoken to successful businesswomen to find out how they have managed, they have decided to open themselves up to receiving ideas and help. As a result , they are just as open to giving the same support to others.

If you imagine that the system is like a plant, it will need air, light and water to live. If you keep it in a dark room, deprived of light, air and water, it will die. Your system is the same. You may think that you are protecting it, by keeping everyone out of your business, by not sharing your vulnerabilities, concerns, successes and triumphs, but actually you will be depriving it of the benefit of others' diversity of experience and views, which can emerge as shoots of ideas, support and challenge. I am constantly amazed by the kindness of others when they are given the opportunity and even my own giving surprises me, when I am allowed to have the space to support or share success with someone. You don't need to go overboard with this. Leave a plant out in harsh sunlight and its leaves can become burnt and dry, its soil can be drowned by the rain, the leaves battered and the wind can tear it from its roots. You have to let a nourishing amount in without overdoing it and you have to let it respire, stretch out into the world and grow.

If, like me, you are not good with plants, this concept can be quite worrying. But I have begun to buy hardier plants, ones that need water and light but don't die without one day's attention. This is also a metaphor for my system, it doesn't collapse if I am working away for a night; you may be better at it. Have at least one plant in your home to remind you of the system that needs to be kept nourished or, if that is too much of a challenge, start with a tree in your garden or one that you see daily that will act as a reminder of your need to keep your system open, nourished and growing.

Two of the women MEs I spoke to had relationships that had broken down. Bernadette's husband had closed his system down and decided not to nourish it anymore, while Sally chose to focus her priorities on work as she had always done and this was not how her husband saw the system working sustainably. Sondra completely acknowledges her husband's role in keeping the system alive, sharing responsibility for the children, supporting and encouraging her and doing the cooking. Although I have concentrated on your role within the system, it is not just your responsibility to nourish it; the others within the system need to be as committed and aware as you are of its delicate and complex nature and the need to keep it alive.

REFLECTION

* How could you share this idea with others?
* How healthy is your system right now?
* What do you need to do to nourish it?
* Who can help?

Aware of your interdependencies

The complex network of interdependencies is enabling. Often it's not until you lose something that you appreciate it. If you have a bout of the flu and you lose your sense of taste, you start to recognise how much that impacts your appetite. Or if you have ever sprained a muscle or broken a bone you start to realise how much you rely on it, not just for balance but also how it connects to other parts of your body. The complex network of interdependencies can work so well it is invisible until we consciously think about taking it away.

ACTION - What makes your system work?

List 5 things that make your system work. It could be: trust, flexibility, organisation, humour, great friends etc.

Now write the sentence below 5 times, inserting a different one of the things that make your system work in the space and completing the sentence

If x was removed from my system, the consequences would be...?

This is a wake-up call to your interdependencies. Celebrate and appreciate the interdependencies within your system and nourish them.

Come up with one small thing you will do to nourish your system and show you appreciate it.

Maybe you're not feeling so independent now. You have the opportunity to acknowledge the system that you have around you which enables you to be ME. You are part of something bigger than yourself, while also being a critical part within it. You are still mistress of your own destiny, just with an increased awareness that your actions will have a reaction.

Chapter 9 - The Real ME

Work is good, provided you do not forget to live

AFRICAN PROVERB

ME at home

With work playing a starring role in your life, it's no wonder that you take it home sometimes, but when you find yourself continuing to act the part offstage you may need to ponder on the impact of that. There are many factors that create the person you are at work: the culture and way things are done in your organisation, which is often an ethos created by the person at the top; your position and what is expected of someone in that role; as well as your past experience of work, role models and mentors. This work persona may be a slightly enhanced version of you, or someone very different, depending on your fit with your work environment. However much you decide to bring of your whole self into work and be authentic, your behaviour is likely to be different to what it would be at home.

For starters, there is often a different language in the workplace, which is easy to slip into at home. Andrea found herself doing just this: "Once, when we were talking about something to do with the children and who makes the decisions I said, 'Yes but I'm really like the leader,' which obviously my husband teased me massively about and still does. I can't remember what the decision was." More appropriate language would be, "I am the mother, the organiser, the person who holds things together," but the language of business slipped in and stood out like a sore thumb. Why? Because it takes away from the emotional and relational connection you have with your family. Remember when you first started your role, the work jargon of most organisations is alienating at first; unless you partner works in the same field, it will be like you are speaking another language to them.

You may have to present yourself differently at work. If this is the case, you need to be flexible enough to shift back when you are at home. Often, it's not that you don't want to, it's just that you haven't consciously left that work persona at the front door, which is even more challenging when you work from home, as an increasing number of women do. If you are in a senior role, it's likely that you will be exuding a self-assuredness and confidence in order to help those who work with you feel secure. If you have a leadership coach, the sessions will provide a space for your vulnerabilities to come out, but your home space can also provide it. Carl Rogers, who founded Person-Centred Therapy, said that Acceptance, Congruence and Empathy otherwise known as (ACE) need to be in place for a helping environment or conversation; I keep them at the heart of my leadership coaching practice. I think these same qualities need to be present for you to feel safe enough to allow yourself to be vulnerable. You need to feel accepted as you are, know that whoever you share with is being genuine and honest, empathises, thinks highly of you and wants the best for you. Is that present for you?

REFLECTION

* When was the last time you allowed yourself to feel vulnerable?

* What made it possible to do so?

* Are you dropping your work persona when you get home? If not, should you?

* If you work from home, how do you shape-shift from work persona to home?

Being your 'shoes-off' self

When you get home and kick off your shoes and wiggle your toes, and become your shoes-off self, who are you and how different are you from the person who was in the office a short time before? There are characteristics and preferences for behaviour that make you uniquely you, this combination of qualities can be referred to as your persona. How aware are you of the difference between your work and home persona, what aspects of your personality do you emphasise or play down in order to be professional, fit in and carry out your role well? In Chapter 7, I referred to personality questionnaires based on the work of Carl Jung, to help leaders consider their personality preferences and communication approach.

It takes one of your most precious commodities, energy, to emphasise and play down aspects of who you are at work. You need to replenish this energy by switching off regularly and being your shoes-off self - and you need to be aware enough of who that person is in order to be able to do so.

Here are some simplified questions to help you to start to consider what's different between your work and home persona, what aspects of your personality you put energy into at work and which aspects you are forgetting to drop when you walk into your home.

 ACTION - Being you at home

Start by spending a couple of minutes thinking of your shoes-off self, when you are most comfortable and relaxed at home. What are you like, how do you engage with those around you, how do you make decisions and think things through?

Then think about work and tick one of each pair of statements that you agree with or write it down in your journal.

	✓
I am more sociable and outgoing at work, wanting to be at the centre of things, speaking up frequently.	
I am more introverted at work, keeping myself to myself and preferring to work alone, preferring email rather than face-to-face contact where possible to enable me to reflect on my responses.	
I am more visionary at work, looking at the big picture and the long-term.	
I am more detail-focused at work, ensuring the i's are dotted and t's crossed, than I would be with home affairs.	
I am more compassionate in my decision making, stepping into the shoes of colleagues, staff and customers.	
I am more detached at work, more able to make objective decisions based on facts and criteria rather than emotions.	
I am more methodical, organised and structured at work.	
I am more last-minute, frenetic and driven by deadlines at work.	

The statements that you have ticked suggest where you are using energy to emphasise or play down aspects of your personality, which is likely to be serving you well. So it's just about remembering to relax this energy when you are at home. For example, if you find that you are putting a lot of energy into being extroverted at work, being vocal in meetings, ensuring that you are socialising with your staff, when you get home you can just tell yourself that it's OK to have quiet time. If you drive home, you could do this by spending a couple of minutes in the car before you step into your home, just allowing yourself to return to that more relaxed person.

There are many ways that you can put in place some sort of ritual to help you, such as changing out of work clothes or taking off make up, or it might just be the first cup of coffee that marks the transition from work to home life.

Everyone needs some downtime

The constant need to be on top of everything: home, work, children, relationship, means that there may be little time to unwind, but even if you are not compelled to have more downtime for your sanity, you may need some before things start to unravel elsewhere. Can you afford to have time off or have your career derailed due to stress, illness or exhaustion?

Through our coaching sessions, one of my female clients came to the stark realisation that her best self was displayed at work and her worst at home. Does this resonate with you? When you give everything to work, you can have nothing left in your reserves for home life. Down time is necessary so that those you care about most don't get the frayed edges of your personality.

As a professional woman, sadly it is true that you are still judged on your appearance. The unkempt, tired look resulting from little downtime will unfortunately not help you to be taken seriously and promoted. Your downtime will enable you to look and feel your best and give you a space where you can take the makeup off, wear the comfy slippers and rejuvenate. A space to be uncensored, un-politically correct, un-judged. I dare you to tell me that you don't need that!

If you're good at something, you naturally want to do more of it, especially if it's being rewarded. It's easy to be seduced into being a workaholic, particularly if you are self-employed. The enticement, temptation and charm of work is something to be resisted, particularly when it takes priority over all other aspects of your life. Remember the perspective on happiness was balance, so how could you balance out this work life so that it doesn't take over? What's the opposite of what you do at work?

Whatever it is: Book it, Plan it, Make Space for it and Do it.

You are still a woman

Stop acting like a woman and people will stop treating you like one. Yes you are in a traditionally male role as ME, you may even work in a male-dominated environment and I am sure you interact with men regularly, but you really don't have to become one; you can be ME on your own terms.

No doubt you can be your own worst enemy, seeking equality and being very capable, you may decline the assistance of men. Victoria recalls staying at a hotel for business and coming out with her suitcase, a gentleman offered to help her take her luggage down some stairs and she declined the offer, her inner-voice telling her that she was a tough, independent woman who didn't need help. Later she saw the man again and he said: "At least I can hold the door open for you this time," and it hit her that by letting him help, he was feeling good about himself, rather than taking anything away from her. She also thought about the fact that actually, if all women continue to decline help, one day they just won't be asked anymore. There are times when it's OK to acknowledge that you are a woman and can accept help, support and kindness from men. After all we are different, and that is to be embraced.

Like the aspects of your personality that you may emphasise or play down for work, you may also be doing something similar with your femininity. Rhonda works in a male dominated environment and I suspect that she has played down her femininity at work to fit in, while Andrea has found her femininity an asset, being self-employed, and has worked in more typically female sectors.

The qualities of being ME combine the masculine and feminine, if you find that the masculine is taking over in a way that is not good for you, you may need to rekindle your femininity. For example, if you turn your bedroom activity into a military exercise, your spouse probably won't be interested .

REFLECTION

If you were to rekindle your femininity, what would be happening that's not happening now? A cuddle, date-time, an image consultant, or an investment in new lingerie?

ACTION - Rekindling your femininity

Do something feminine, even if it's not you, such as read a romantic novel, watch a romantic comedy. Perhaps, if you wear more tailored suits for work, buy a more feminine outfit, have a makeover or pamper session. Do you feel different?

Feeling like the man *and* woman of the house?

Being ME can make you feel like the man and woman of the house. You *can* need without being needy. Your huge capacity to be capable means that you are demonstrating that you can do everything a man can do and everything a woman can do. This is fantastic! You are also demonstrating that you do not need anyone; not so fantastic. What do you do when you are not needed? Go and find somewhere where you are needed? Do your own thing? You need to show that you need others without being needy. You need to create space for others to contribute. Femi describes how her husband now just cooks the dinner instead of waiting for her to get home and ask what he should cook.

The experience in the world of work can be quite a masculine one. We can bring those attributes home with us. Rhonda said that she was the leader to her husband, who scoffed at her. Another said that she was project-managing her home. Although in reality she probably does do these things, those around her don't need to hear it. Don't turn those who matter around you into employees. However good a boss you are, ultimately your staff will do what you ask because there might be some financial and career reward at the end of it.

Create some sunshine and your femininity will shine through. If you are not feeling good about things, you don't feel good about yourself. What creates sunshine for you? More fun, social life, shopping, dates, losing weight, exercising, meditation, praying, a meal, a movie. The more relaxing and enjoyable times you have, the more likely you will be able to get in touch with your femininity. It is usually the drudgery of life that makes you become a man and a woman in one.

Build in regular rewards - don't do it all, even though we know that you can - *wink*.

Value your femininity

Your femininity has unique value. You may have to spend a lot of your time describing yourself in male terms; I notice it a lot in my conversations with women leaders. This results in you no longer being able to recall and value your feminine qualities, such as cherishing relationships, emotional intelligence and collaboration, which are valued highly in the workplace and are now considered an integral and important part of leadership.

Because these precious attributes can come naturally to you, you often don't value them as you should. When was the last time you thought about how useful it is to be a woman and the unique qualities you bring?

ACTION - Your feminine traits

Look at the list below. Do not dismiss them because they are not valued in the workplace; could they be the part of you that you have pushed to the side because of your role as ME? How would you once have described yourself? Could you embrace that description in a positive way for you again?

Circle below or note down in your journal three words that sound like you now, or in the past.

Activate the meaning of those words in you by remembering how they have been positively valued by others.

Choose one feminine quality to demonstrate daily over the next 30 days in order to bring it back into being part of who you are. Note it in the front inside cover of your journal, so it doesn't get lost among the pages.

Gentle	Yielding	Close	Motherly
Sensitive	Soft	Quiet	Receptive
Compassionate	Nurturing	Passive	Homemaker
Sympathetic	Graceful	Family oriented	Inwardly oriented
Tender	Communicative	Responsive	Relationship oriented
Understanding	Intuitive	Cooperative	Loving
Warm	Emotional	Conservative	Kind

Being you is good enough

What's the point of being ME if you don't get to enjoy it? The income earning is important, but is it more important than your relationship? Perhaps you have it out of kilter.

Remember your system and its interdependencies. Being the boss, manager, leader or professional all the time can impact your system adversely through your actions. If you find yourself complaining that your partner doesn't think for themselves or that they don't take the initiative, think about your part in enabling the situation to occur. Femi described her husband waiting for her to be home to decide what the children should have for dinner. This was not because he wasn't capable, but because he had lost his sense of power to take the initiative. She realised that she had to step back and encourage him to make decisions, even if they weren't the ones she would have made, so that she wouldn't be the one doing everything.

Being ME will change you, and so will all your other experiences and development opportunities, but you need to be aware of when to switch it off. When I first trained to be a coach, I found myself coaching all the time, attempting to coach neighbours and friends to hone my skills. I soon realised that this was not appropriate, that people just wanted me and that if they wanted coaching, they'd ask for it. Being you is good enough at home.

You may have found the exercises in this chapter liberating. How are you feeling? Good, I hope.

Chapter 10 - Enjoying ME

You might not admit anything you discover about yourself in this chapter to anyone else, but please, at least admit it to yourself. My coaching code of confidentiality stands; I am happy to keep it between us *wink!*.

Just like being ME has been a trigger, catalyst or starting point for increased complexity in your life... *how could you forget*... so it has been for a number of benefits that you might not readily admit. Are you scratching your head, wondering what I'm talking about? Well I think you've been afraid of your ego getting out of control, but this pride plays a transformational role in helping you sustain and renew your inner strength while being ME. It's only normal to be attracted to feeling good. Knowing that something about being ME is making you feel that way is excellent self-knowledge that you should hold dear.

I am sure if I was writing for men most wouldn't need so much persuasion about pride in their role!

You enjoy having a voice

If you won the lottery today or your partner landed a top job that brought in a high income that meant you wouldn't need to work anymore, would you gladly give up work and being ME? Your answer off the top of your head might be: "Hell Yes!" but what about the answer that's lurking there in the pit of your stomach? It just might surprise you.

Even though the weighty responsibility, constant juggling and nagging guilt may be a challenge, the truth is you enjoy what it gives you. Your position at work and being ME at home can provide you with such wonderful gifts of equality, power, status, a sense of contributing, the ability to make an impact, a plethora of choices and access to a world outside of the home. Hands up if you want to give that up?... I thought not.

When you've always been ME like Sondra and Sally, you don't know what it's like not to have a voice. Whereas when it is a relatively new arrangement, like Andrea, you can become acutely aware that your voice is more powerfully given and more accepted because of your role as ME. In an ideal world you would be listened to anyway, but part of the payback for being ME is that you will at the very least be heard and have an integral part in decision making. Who wants all the work without the perks? Often women who are not MEs have an equal contribution to make but don't give it so forcefully, as they don't feel in a position to do so.

It's very much like having a senior professional role at work or being brought in as an expert consultant, people listen to you because:

1. You expect to be listened to
2. You see yourself as equal
3. You recognise your own contribution

It's less about them and all about you.

You enjoy making decisions

Knowing that you have the ability to make decisions without consultation is a great feeling, acting on it might not be. As we said in Chapter 7 - communication is critical, so making major decisions without discussion is not necessarily a good thing, but knowing you can is.

All of the women MEs I have spoken to have a passion for learning and developing themselves no matter their age, the investment in your continuous professional development and personal development would be more difficult to justify if you weren't ME. But as ME you can give good reasons for why your development is a high priority.

Rhonda says: "One of my biggest drivers is my personal development and so going to work and having the opportunities that are at work, gives me those chances to develop further.

If I'm not at work, I know I am developing, but it's at a much slower pace and very, very differently and not in the direction that I'd probably want to go in. I suppose when I do work, I've got a lot more, I earn more, so you've got a lot more choice in all sorts of ways too."

Femi says: "If you want to take the pressure off and control those little things, get a cleaner, get a cook, get someone to do the gardening, get a nanny. You have a lot more time and life is much easier, it makes a big difference."

Would you discuss these forms of help for your household if you were not ME? These are often the things which are impossible for you to keep doing while you are in that role. You can have a major say in the decision making around gaining this household support and are likely to be giving another woman - maybe even a ME - a job in the process.

Connie found that regular trips to the hairdresser were her saviour when she was finding it particularly tough; it was a safe haven for her, which she saw as an investment in her sanity rather than a cost. The reality is that having to ask for things like attending a training course, getting a cleaner or going to the hairdresser, means that you often don't. Being in your position, you only need to ask if you want to.

You enjoy the power

We talked about power a little in Chapter 3, when we discussed the impact of your financial independence. If you recall, I said that power is everywhere and is not necessarily a bad thing. Your boss has power due to her position, however you may hold the power when she needs something done that only you can deliver. Be careful not to wield this power over others.

Using the power that you hold as MF. alongside the values that you identified in Chapter 1, means that you can make a significant positive impact. Whether that is by having more influence or making a significant contribution at work, in your home or community, you have the choice to be able to do so.

To know you have the power means you can distribute it. If you recall, Connie has agreed that her husband should control the finances because he's good at it, she was able to do this because he had the skills in the first place. Connie also talked about the power that she now has in her senior role, she sees that she can now influence policy in the way young people are taught. Power is not a bad thing unless it is abused, it is always present anyway and the balance of it moves around all the time.

How can you harness this power positively? Perhaps you can use it to equalise your relationship as Andrea did in the example in Chapter 3, where she felt that you need to earn more than your partner in order to have an equal voice. Alternatively, you could be a powerful role model to your children and others to show them how to go out into the world, as Sally put it. This power is to be savoured - like good wine and chocolate - in moderation.

 **ACTION - I can**

In your journal, complete this sentence at least 3 times, more if you can:

Because of my power I CAN...

Because of my power I CAN...

Because of my power I CAN...

What came out for you, was there a theme?

Admit it to me only, what is it about being ME that you relish?

Empowerment and freedom

You usually ooze confidence. You have freedom from the traditional idea of dependence, even though you know that we are all interdependent from our work together in the last chapter. There is nothing more attractive to be around than a confident and relatively independent woman. Whether friend, colleague or partner, the inner glow of confidence attracts others like moths to a flame. Have you noticed it in yourself?

The value that society puts on the family income and status means that when you know that you are contributing to the nice house, education, food, holidays, car etc., society tells you that this is a good thing. Although I won't argue that being ME is a big responsibility, knowing that you are significantly contributing, if not keeping your family afloat, must make you feel good.

You are a capable individual and you should have already become very aware of this. Work gives you freedom; you are not usually tied to the house, although you may be home based, you can exist as your own person. This is different to working part-time within school hours to contribute to the family income, because that demonstrates a different priority, you are then a working mum, not a mum who is ME, with all that entails.

Feeling positive

The positive focus born out of making your corner of the world work, means that you minimise issues. As ME you don't have to dwell on barriers, you can't let things get in your way as people are relying on you. As such, this drives you, helping you not to get stuck in pot-holes along the way, the typical barriers to success for women, like stereotyping, lack of mentors, lack of visibility and myths about your ability to manage your work/life balance. Instead, you dispute those by your very existence.

As such you are likely to be creating your own path, like Rhonda, who is married with children, a senior manager in her organisation, or Andrea and Sally, who decided to take the entrepreneurial route.

Continue to stay positive and future focused, and minimise your focus on problems.

Sense of accomplishment

You enjoy the sense of accomplishment outside as well as inside the family system.

When I asked women MEs for a different descriptor for the term ME, one that came up was 'successful and accomplished'. This is what *you* are and one of the things that helps you to sustain being ME is that sense of accomplishment.

A sense of success and accomplishment leads to more of the same and helps you to continue to grow and develop and be ambitious for yourself and your family.

Rhonda knows that she wouldn't have enjoyed a lesser role at work and in the home: "But the funny thing is, if I had gone back to work part-time I would have had to take a demotion because it wouldn't have been possible to do my work part-time. If I'd not done that then I know that I would think more choice had been taken away from me." The experience of work can be laden with reward and sense of achievement which, understandably, is not something that you would want to let go of.

REFLECTION

* Think of a particularly good week where you worked.
* What were the highlights at home and work?
* What does that tell you about what you really enjoy?
* *Shhhh*, I won't tell...!
* Do you now know what you love about being ME? It has its plus points doesn't it?

Chapter 11 - Invest in ME

Respect yourself, you will get it back.

TUNISIAN PROVERB

You may have noticed a theme throughout this book and it is that the key to making your corner of the world work as ME is YOU. In many ways, working through the cycles of reflection and action within the chapters will be a nurturing experience for you and I hope you have already made some changes which create more space for you to notice, awaken and look after yourself.

However, I am sure you still have more work to do to ensure that you don't slip back into old habits and can continue to make YOU a priority.

Do you remember I mentioned the Superwoman Syndrome way back in Chapter 6? I am sure it struck a chord with you, staying up late or waking early to catch up on work and not invade family time, trying to be all things to all people and be everywhere at the same time, ultimately spreading yourself so thin that you are almost opaque. This is why you need to spend time on you, firstly to notice that you are doing this and secondly, to renew and revitalise.

When I am away for work for a few days and my husband is with my daughter, he is always exhausted on my return. When I ask why, he says that he has been listening out for my daughter at night just in case she has a bad dream or needs him. This means that when I am there he is relying on me to sleep lightly and wake for her if needed and so, sleeps soundly himself. Women are so different, we take on that responsibility no matter what. This is just one way in which our responsibilities are added to; even when we are sleeping we have a role in the home!

When you try to emulate men in the way you live out being ME, this can create added stress and tension. The image portrayed by many professional women is that they can do it all and that nothing has to give when juggling family, work and being ME. I understand why you might do this. Ultimately you don't want to perpetuate stereotypes of women being unreliable and unstable. This doesn't help other women though, it just makes them feel inadequate and may even set them up to fail. How do you present yourself? As a woman who does it all or a woman who needs support to do it all? Perhaps it depends on the audience.

The combination of trying to do it all, a relentless role in life, even as you sleep, and the presentation of yourself as managing it all with ease is a gruelling regime. If it were an Olympic sport it would take many years to train for and would probably last twenty minutes as an event; but this is your life!

A dangerous message

Not prioritising *you* sends out a dangerous message that you're not important.

What message are you giving to others if you don't prioritise you? You are giving permission for others to take you for granted. Yes I know that you think everyone should know how busy you are, but actually because you are so capable, people will continue to give you more and more responsibility until you say: 'No'. Like your closet that you continue to fill with clothes, you may tell yourself at some point, 'I must sort out the clothes I am not going to wear again,' but you don't do it, until one day the closet collapses and you realise that it was one dress too far and recognise that you have to spend time re-evaluating what should actually be in there.

People will push and pull for your attention and energy from all angles if you do not consciously work on this and you'll collapse just like the closet if you do not give this area of your life attention. Instead, replace this behaviour with regular checking-in and re-evaluating, so you don't leave it to breaking point to prioritise *you*.

One of my clients has an elderly mother that she looks after in her home, as well as working full time. She commendably prioritises her mother and at times becomes exhausted. She is giving everything to work and to her mother and nothing to herself. The onus is on you here, because others' perspective is their reality; if you appear to be coping, it's unlikely that others will question it. You are the only one who really knows how you feel and what you need, so stop waiting for others to tell you. They will only notice when it becomes extreme, why wait when you have it in your power to prioritise *you* now?

If you were teaching someone to drive, you would show them how to do it well and attempt not to teach them any of the bad habits that you have accumulated over the years. You would model your best self. In the same way, as ME you need to model this best self to other women and your children, in order for them to understand how to make the best of their situation. If you want them to have a good sense of wellbeing, to feel physically and mentally healthy and vital, then you should place it high on the agenda for yourself.

REFLECTION - Treat yourself as a friend

You may find it easier to prioritise others rather than yourself. If you had a friend who was exactly like you, what advice would you give her about treating herself well? What gift would you give to her that she would benefit from?

Give this gift to yourself.

ACTION - Schedule it

I know that scheduling wellbeing or fun time can sound counterintuitive, especially if you like to be spontaneous, but if you don't schedule it, it won't happen, other things will take precedence. Slot a space for *you* into the diary like any other important event and keep that time sacred, however short.

Below are some things that you can do to prioritise *you*. They are in no particular order - choose what's right for you and be inspired to come up with your own ideas.

Enjoy the moment - you can spend a lot of time rushing from one place to the other, but how about enjoying the moments in between? There are gaps of time, when you may be travelling or waiting. I have ninety minutes on Saturday mornings where my daughter is in a class, I love this time and use it to wander around window shopping, read my book or have a coffee and watch the world go by. There are many more sensible things I could do, like the weekly food shop, or catch up on my work, or rush home and clean the house, but I choose to prioritise me during that time and it sets me up for the weekend. When are the moments that you could enjoy?

Go for a massage - just a thirty minute massage helps you get back in touch with your body, relax your muscles and quieten the mind. You might be able to schedule this in before, or after work, or even at lunchtime. If you have more time, book a half day's holiday from work and treat yourself to a leisurely lunch as well.

Hotel gym or spa - if you are away for business, take advantage of the hotel gym and spa instead of just being holed up in your room answering emails or flicking through TV channels. A quick swim or just a jacuzzi connects you with the healing power of water. One of the services busy professional women take up with me is one-to-one holistic coaching; pampering and personal development at the same time. Coaching takes place at a five star spa, clients use the facilities, have lunch, followed by a coaching session. They find it useful for re-evaluating goals and generating ideas for the future and leave with a sense of wellness.

Professional and personal development - the process of learning something new will keep you feeling fresh and curious about life. This can be investing in an industry publication, reading books like this one, engaging a coach or mentor, perhaps even attending a training programme or conference. If you are self-employed you have more freedom; schedule a day a quarter for your personal development, whatever that is for you. Alternatively, there is a wealth of material on the internet you can access and a range of online courses that you can engage with at your own pace.

Exercise - getting your heart pumping and your body moving circulates the oxygen around your body and contributes to your sense of happiness as well as health. Build exercise into your life; it doesn't have to be two hours at the gym each day unless that is what you like to do. It can be walking up the escalator rather than just standing on it, walking in the park, playing on the games console with your children, going cycling as a family, attending yoga classes, dance classes, sport classes like karate, boxing, badminton, purchasing an exercise machine or just a skipping rope or hula hoop. The list is endless and as easy as you want to make it.

Eat well - a good combination of healthy and nutritious food is important to keep your body and mind processing at its best. Even if you are in a rush, there are many healthy options available to you, like good soups packed with nutrients and energy packed salads. Don't overdo the stimulants like coffee and alcohol which will adversely affect your metabolism. There's nothing wrong with treats, just try to take the healthy option 80% of the time.

Seek flexibility - are there opportunities to work from home once in a while, particularly after being away on business or the completion of an intense working period? Working from home usually means that you have more time for you as you are not travelling and are usually engaged in fewer meetings. This is good time for reflection and, as you are more in control of your day, you can incorporate *you* time.

Stilling the mind - meditation, mindfulness, focusing, yoga, are all great ways of quietening the mind in order to feel a sense of calm and control. If you notice that you are beginning to get irate over small things that wouldn't have bothered you previously, this is probably what you need. You can invest in audio and video recordings so that you can do this at home, or attend classes. Some coaches, like me, provide enlightenment coaching, which incorporates meditation, to help clients to clear their mind and centre themselves before the talking starts. Most activities can be done in as little as five minutes; the time it takes to make your morning coffee. If you don't do this, small things will send you off the edge. Meditation, boot camps, spas and dog walks can all help.

Floatation therapy - when you have a lot on your mind and you are constantly rushing from one activity to another, even if you want to stop and focus on yourself, sometimes your mind just won't slow down. A way to slow down and deepen your thinking is to book three sessions of floatation therapy at a floatation centre, away from distractions. This calming sensory deprivation, while immersed in warm salt water, will help you to find a relaxed and healing state and it will help to still the inner critic and the mass of thoughts that go through your head a trillion times a second, creating space for new thoughts and feelings. It's a wonderful experience which only takes an hour and helps to boost your sense of wellbeing, resourcefulness and perspective. While in the tank, you can listen to calming music or pose one question to yourself that you would like to answer - it really works. Three one hour sessions will usually make a big difference.

Rekindle an old hobby - doing something for pure pleasure probably doesn't happen that much in your busy life. Indulge in a hobby; perhaps you used to paint, write, sew or visit art galleries before life got so hectic, or perhaps there is something you always wanted to do like baking, photography or learning a new language? The good thing about hobbies is that they fit around everything else; they are a way of integrating more pleasure into your life and expanding your horizons.

And some quickies:

Buy yourself some flowers or a plant to remind yourself of the beauty around you and liven up your surroundings.

Buy a non work-related magazine that interests you and read it cover to cover.

Go to a coffee shop or restaurant on your own and indulge in people watching or reading a good book, along with some good food and drink.

Call an old friend and have a good gossip.

Go and see a film you've been meaning to see at the cinema.

Have a luxurious bath, with lit candles. Moisturise and have an early night.

Sing along to your favourite tune.

You are only limited by your imagination. Choose an activity to schedule in the diary for you; something that you can do within the next week. It can be from this list, or you may have others. This is the start of remembering to invest in you.

Your early warning system

This space for attention on *you*, creates an early warning system to notice how you are feeling, how things are going, aches and pains and patterns that are occurring in your life - the niggling issues that are at the back of your mind, taking up time and energy. It wasn't until Victoria went out with a friend who was another ME for lunch, that she realised what was bothering her. Her friend mentioned that her partner always said how happy he was that she could bring in the income and Victoria realised that her partner had never said that and that actually, she felt quite unappreciated in her role and this was something that she would need to address.

No doubt there were other signs that things weren't right for Victoria, perhaps her body was telling her through aching shoulders, tension headaches or break-outs. Maybe her relationships and personal life were deteriorating, or were lacking intimacy. Or possibly she was burying herself in work unable to switch off from it, to escape from the reality of what was going on around her.

When you are in the grip of pressure, problems or uncertainty, you don't always realise it. Investing in yourself helps you to become aware and notice. By doing this you will be able to refocus and prioritise what is important. The investment in *you* creates space to notice, to think, generate ideas and for change to happen.

When do your best thoughts and ideas emerge? I'm guessing it's when you wake up in the morning and when you are relaxed, happy and playful; but how often are you in that state? For Victoria, she needed this lunch date with her friend; it created the space to notice what she was not saying, so that she could go on to have a conversation with her husband. Without the space to notice, it may have bubbled away, culminating in a shocking eruption or worse, slowly eroding her relationships.

Investing in you is the only way to avoid the pitfalls of being ME, such as: trying to do it all, relationship problems and becoming a workaholic.

Take the time to notice.

You are the jam

You are the centre of your world, holding it up; without you it all falls down. If you are not happy, no one in your family is. There is no doubt that women hold the family together. You are the jam in the family sandwich, you bind, provide comfort and are colourful. Think about the lonely pieces of dry neglected bread without their jam filling, that's what they will be like if you don't find a way to be happy with yourself.

Think longer term, can you really keep going as you are?

What are the signs that things aren't going right for you? Are they physical? Are they in your relationships? Is work suffering?

Spending time on you is not about absolute balance. So I am not saying here that if you spend thirty minutes at work, you must spend thirty minutes with your family and thirty minutes on you. The balance is what works for you. Think of a seesaw; if two girls sit on either side who weigh exactly the same, it doesn't move. Instead, it is best if their weights are different and they compensate for that. The girl who weighs more will not be pushing down too hard, the girl who weighs less will be giving it a bit more effort. This is what balance looks like, the constant adapting and taking into consideration of what you need to do. If the girl who weighs more decides to not to consider the fact the other could get hurt, and if the lighter girl doesn't put in the effort, the other will be doing all the work and become exhausted.

You are the fulcrum of your family system. The problem is that sometimes you are the girl doing all the work and don't realise until your legs begin to hurt, at that point the game is over; career, health, wealth and relationships are all suffering.

You need reserves and spending time on you helps you to access them and helps you to build resilience. Knowing what has helped you get where you are means that if the ground disappears from under you, you know you'll survive.

However on a practical level, you should be thinking about your safety nets, such as healthcare and savings.

Sustaining ME

The responsibility, although empowering, can be draining for some women. You need to keep being good at your job to maintain your position. Your work should be valued, not as an interruption, but as the thing that helps and brings you what you want. So it follows that it is not something you want to take for granted. If you want to progress in your career, you need to continue to develop your skills, experience, knowledge and networks.

You will need to show that work is important to you and not something that takes you away from where you'd really like to be. If it isn't, you are likely to consider changing your role or profession, because as the ME you'll be spending a lot of your life working and you don't want that time to be unfulfilling.

To sustain your stamina for your career, it will be crucial for you to refill and re-energise regularly. If you don't do this, small things will send you off the edge. Take the time to recognise what you need. Victoria found that she had to book regular holidays to maintain her balance, while for Connie, using a hairdresser and employing a cleaner were her saviours.

What's your plan for staying on top of your career? The investment in you should be professional as well as personal.

ACTION - Plan for staying on top of your career

Put a career development plan together for yourself, some suggested headings are:

Areas for development;

Timeframe;

Milestones/Actions;

Outcomes.

Below are some ideas of things you might want to do to stay on top of your career:

Learning

Developing

Keep being ambitious

Innovating

Managing and leading well

Maintaining good working relationships

Growing your network

Seeking out a mentor

Engaging a coach

Picking yourself up

It's OK to have a down day and when you do, wallow like a hippo in mud - it's all good.

I know that it's not all sunshine and rainbows, sometimes you'll feel sad, you have permission to do so. You might have to paint a happy face on for work, but wherever you feel most comfortable, you should be able to dwell for a short time. Decide how long you want to give yourself; an hour, a day? Indulge yourself, cry, scream, whatever you need to do, because you know it won't last forever.

When the time is right, make sure you have strategies for extricating yourself. It could be seeing friends, watching a feel-good movie, listening to your favourite uplifting music, whatever will bring back your happy spirit.

You may be tempted to ignore the learning from this chapter as not a major priority. That would be a mistake. At least one action should have come from your list of actions and reflections, if not you should review the chapter. Prioritise you!

Chapter 12 - Share with ME

Come here my beloved
Come give me a kiss.
There is a new law
Which says we must embrace each other.

ZULU of SOUTH AFRICA

The act of sharing your experience is a way for you to embrace other women who are also MEs, it's an invaluable opportunity to learn from each other.

It feels strange to me that I need to encourage you to share, I know people think that women talk all the time and that all we do is share (some would say, gossip) but it seems that there are some things we don't talk about that we should. This lack of sharing outside of your small family unit, often just you, your partner and children, has led to you feeling quite alone. In addition, the lack of practice in sharing means that even now, when you may want some support and help you have lost the art and skill of sharing.

I want to tell you that you are not alone; you have me, for starters! I want you to know that what you say will have value to other women MEs.

Oliver Wendell Holmes said: 'Many ideas grow better when transplanted into another mind than in the one where they sprung up.' The act of sharing, talking and being with other women is an opportunity for you to become clear about your identity as ME, to share ideas that can help you and make you feel resourceful. The ideas that will come to you through conversation and later, reflection, could make radical improvements to the way you do things and in how you experience the world.

In addition, you know that as a professional woman it never hurts to grow your circle of contacts and network.

I want to help you to plan and decide how you might share with other women and men when you are ready to do so, so they can benefit from your knowledge, experience and the knowledge you have gained from working through this book and in your life.

Moving from me to we

I am not criticising your family unit, I have one too, and it is the centre of my world, but what it can do is make you think in a very individualistic way: it's all about me and my family situation, instead of the fact that being ME is about women and us. The women I have spoken to have been kind enough to share their wisdom and experience, the lessons that they have learned along the way. If they were just thinking of themselves, they would have been too concerned about exposing their lives or thinking about what else they could be doing with their valuable time. Instead, they invested in womankind and I thank them. Could you do the same?

Rhonda has taken the plunge, "I'm looking at starting a support group within my own company to try and tease out who those people are, because I haven't found them if they're there."

You might start smaller than this, it could be just broaching the subject with some trusted friends.

REFLECTION

When have you stepped from me to we in the past? Perhaps you've engaged in community, charity, church or spiritual work or you've come together as a family unit, or been united as an organisation.

How did it feel?

Being part of something is powerful, isn't it?!

Sharing lessons learnt

When I interviewed the women featured in this book, I asked them for three lessons from their experience of being ME that they would share with other women in the same position. A few overlapped, but many didn't, some also contradicted each other which is interesting. For me, this highlights the uniqueness of each woman's experience. The lessons learned summarise the themes of this book and would not have been unlocked without my sharing and seeking them out. They are listed below for you to benefit from and share:

Gender isn't relevant, if you're good at what you do, it speaks for itself, whether you're a woman or not.

You must be versatile, you need to flex and adapt your approach according to the audience and situation without losing sight of who you are.

Rhonda sums it up: "I probably end up being about a thousand different people in my work and private life. But there's always the common denominator. So it's knowing how to play it and having versatility. So, you know, one door may close but if you're good, another one will open."

You're part of a system, and that's going to make a difference to what you do and how you do it because they are all interdependent.

Andrea brought this to the table when she said: "So even though I'm a ME, I've needed the support of others to do that and it's never finished. So you think you've cracked it and then something else comes along."

Be resilient, cautious and tenacious Bernadette is the epitome of these qualities, she lost her job two years ago. It took her five months and two thousand applications before she got another one, but she persevered.

Learn to compromise and have regular discussions, for the health of your relationship.

Believe that you are at least equal all the time.

Don't put your life in the hands of an organisation, develop yourself and invest in yourself and you'll always do well. Knowledge is crucial for success; learn, read, ask questions.

Respect money, be sensible.

Seek a strong network of colleagues and friends, feel comfortable with asking others for help.

It's OK to get things wrong, as long as you learn from it.

Weigh up patience Vs instant gratification, we all want it now, but sometimes we have to consider the long game.

It's OK to take a risk at any age.

Don't try and do it all, risk not doing what you think you ought to do.

Give quality time to those who are important to you.

Get support, contract out as much as you can.

REFLECTION

* What do you think of these lessons, were they worth sharing?
* Which lessons most resonate with you?
* Which will you act upon?
* Which of them will you share with someone who could benefit?
* What other lessons will you learn?

You are in good company

If you have ever bought a car, you'll be familiar with the feeling of suddenly noticing so many more of the make, model and colour of vehicle that you are driving. You see what you look for; you never had a reason to notice that vehicle before. Maybe that's the reason you are unlikely to know many other MEs, but when you start looking, I am sure they'll reveal themselves to you and you'll realise that they are everywhere.

The more that women in the public eye demonstrate their ability to be MEs, the easier it will be for you. Had you noticed the growing number of women around you in a similar situation?

When you choose to be open about being ME, other women will share too.

ACTION - Know more MEs

* List the women MEs that you know.
* List the women you think may be MEs and try to find out if they are.

- ✳ Set yourself a target, I will meet x number of women MEs in the next x days.

- ✳ How will you do it? Ask more questions, let people know more about your situation, attend more places, events, online events, where you have the potential of meeting women MEs.

You have more to gain

When coaching women leaders, I have found that my acts of self-disclosure used appropriately - such as sharing a work experience that wasn't good for me - helps my clients to open up. The act of opening yourself up to being vulnerable usually reaps rewards.

When you open up about your situation, it will allow others to feel comfortable to do the same. Just because you are ME, you don't have to be macho, you can be emotionally intelligent without being soft and fluffy.

Rhonda says, "I would never have gone to a women-only group before, I would have never done anything like that, but I realise now that I should do, not just because of what I can get out of it but what I can give to other people."

Still not convinced? I suggest some reflection on what's at the heart of the issue, work through the questions below:

REFLECTION

- ✳ What experience and knowledge do you have that you think other MEs could learn from?

- ✳ Think about different experiences of sharing, did you get what you wanted?

- ✳ How do/did you ensure you get what you need?

* What needs to be in place?

* When you think about sharing, do you notice what happens? Some people will feel lighter, but others will have had a negative experience of sharing, how can you make this experience as good as it gets?

* What's standing in your way? How do you remove it?

How will you share?

You need to find the right group for you. The word 'network' may make you cringe. Fears and excuses may arise, such as:

I will be in too much of a clique

I am not a group person

I don't need more friends

I won't fit in

They'll all be more successful/ articulate/ beautiful than me

I don't have the time

Remember the thoughts that raised their heads when we talked about not holding back on your choices in Chapter 2? Note to self: the inner critic is back and speaking in her dulcet tones! You need to push her away again, do this by focusing on your end goal, what it is you want to achieve, rather than what the obstacles to achieving it could be.

Creating opportunities

Although in principle you may be happy to share, you may be having some trouble working out how you do it. The Miracle Question is a powerful questioning technique taken from *Solutions Focused Coaching* which helps you visualise the future you want. I sometimes use this technique with my coaching clients, who say they enjoy it, as it is very positive, fast and focused on the future. By visualising the reality you want, you make it more real for you and therefore more attainable.

 ## ACTION - Visualise it

Read the question below to yourself, where you see the three dots pause for a few seconds and then read on.

Question:

Suppose that while you were asleep tonight, a miracle happens... The miracle is that you know exactly how, when and where to share and support other women MEs... Because you have been asleep, you don't know that the miracle has happened... So when you walk into work, what will you notice that will tell you the miracle actually occurred?

Now answer these questions in your journal.

* What would it look like?
* What would others notice?
* What would they be saying about you?
* What would be happening in your day?
* Who would you be talking to?
* What's your first small step to making this happen? Do it now!

Practical tips on sharing

Existing local networks/groups

Are there existing networks in the local area that you could tap into? Victoria was a member of a speech-making group and used her speeches to talk about her role as ME. She was surprised at the number of women who came up to her afterwards to share their experiences.

Online

There are many online groups you can join or set up easily. The advantage of these is that you can access them anytime and you can also benefit from relative anonymity. You are also likely to get a wider geographical reach.

Professional bodies/ membership organisations

Are you a member of any professional organisations? They often have subgroups and special interest groups. Perhaps you could approach them to set something up? You will already have some common ground which you can build on.

Informal network

You will have amassed an informal network of colleagues and friends. Perhaps you could write five names down and decide to speak to them when it feels appropriate.

Sharing your reflections

You've been noting your reflections in your journal while working your way through this book. How about sharing those reflections through a blog, or writing an article? Or perhaps you used video or images? Again, you could find a channel to share them.

Create your own network

For a guide to setting up your own network, you can download one from www.rockingyourrole.com

Share with me

I am always happy to hear about your experiences and find ways to share them with other women MEs.

Remember that you are part of a system and connected to every woman and man within it; they all have something to learn from you. You don't have to connect with them all, but offering your knowledge and experience to that system means that it might reach someone who really needs it.

You have so much to say and share that can help a fellow ME, it's a crime to keep it to yourself!

 ACTION - Scale it

Emerging from the cycles of action and reflection that you have been guided through, some challenges and solutions about your role as ME will have been revealed. As being ME is ongoing in your life, it will be good for you to plan how you will sustain your ongoing growth and development. By scaling each chapter, you can consider what's still important for you to work on.

Draw 12 scales, with 1 at the left hand side and 10 at the other end, in your journal.

Label the scales 1 to 12:

1. Burying my head in the sand/Dealing with the challenges of being ME
2. Feeling out of control/Feeling that I have choices
3. I can't see the good in my situation/I can see the benefits of being ME
4. I am racked with guilt about being ME/I am guilt-free
5. People's assumptions about my role as ME negatively affect me/I no longer let others' assumptions about me being ME have an impact

6. I am overwhelmed and can't let go of any of my responsibilities/I now know what I *don't* need to do

7. I can't discuss how I feel about being ME and my relationships are suffering as a result/ Good two-way communication is taking place in my important relationships

8. I am fiercely independent and don't need anyone/I recognise my part in the system and that I need support

9. I have lost my femininity as ME, my work persona has taken over/I feel like a woman and can let go of my work persona at home

10. I can't admit that I enjoy anything about being ME/I can admit to myself what I enjoy about being ME

11. I am exhausted and drained and can't make time for me/I regularly schedule in time and activities to invest in my wellbeing

12. I can't talk to anyone about my situation/I am finding ways to share what it's like being ME to support others and myself

Mark where you think you are on each scale.

Any scale you mark closer to the right hand side is an area for you to celebrate, there may still be some work to do but you are definitely getting there.

Any scale you mark closer to left hand side is an area to develop further, revisit those chapters and plan small steps on how to move them a little more to the right.

I have provided an example for you from Gemma's scale. You can see that she still has some work to do around being guilt-free, letting others' assumptions affect her, investing in her well-being and sharing with others.

Gemma's scale

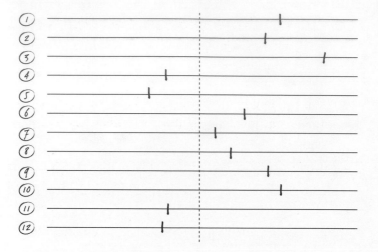

Now you've completed yours, what does this picture tell you about what's important for you to deal with right now?

Note it in your journal and break it down into small steps, do this activity every four to six weeks to keep an eye on how you progress and notice any changes in your situation.

Search in the past for what is good and beautiful. Build your future from there.

PAUL KRUGER

You have come to the end of this guide, but you also have your journal full of insights and reflections to sustain you.

Revisit them and continue to make your corner of the world work by focusing on the areas that are important to you.

Keep Rocking Your Role.

References

Books

African Proverbs & Wisdom, Julia Stewart

Breadwinner Wives and the Men They Marry: How to Have a Successful Marriage While Outearning Your Husband, Randi Minetor

Coming home to Myself, Marion Woodman & Gill Mellick

Female Breadwinners, Suzanne Doyle-Morris

FISH!: A Remarkable Way to Boost Morale and Improve Results, Stephen C. Lundin et al.

I'm OK, You're OK, Thomas A Harris

Presence: Exploring Profound Change in People, Organizations and Society, Senge et al.

Psychology Of Executive Coaching, Bruce Peltier

Solutions Focus, Paul Z Jackson & Mark McKergow

The Artist's Way, Julia Cameron

The Inner Game of Work, Timothy Gallwey

The Origin of Family, Private Property and the State, Frederick Engels

Transitions, William Bridges

You can Heal your Life, Louise Haye

Articles

Balance of financial power in marriage: an exploratory study of breadwinning wives http://onlinelibrary.wiley.com/doi/10.1111/j.1467-954X.1985.tb02439.x/abstract

Big earning wives and the men who love them http://www.somaliaonline.com/community/showthread.php/1439-Big-Earning-Wives-(and-the-Men-Who-Love-Them)

Female Breadwinner Families: The Existence, Persistence and Sources http://ftp.iza.org/dp1308.pdf

It's wrong for women to be breadwinner http://www.tribune.com.ng/sat/index.php/women-affairs/4354-its-wrong-for-women-to-be-breadwinners.html

Rising number of women earn more than their mates http://www.msnbc.msn.com/id/33196583/ns/business-personal_finance/t/rising-number-women-earn-more-mates/

Spending cuts are restoring the old male breadwinner role http://www.guardian.co.uk/society/2010/dec/05/gender-equality-coalition-cuts

The Female Breadwinner: Phenomenological Experience and Gendered Identity in Work/Family Spaces, Rebecca J. Meisenbach http://www.springerlink.com/content/c872j48kj7p7w876/

They Call It the Reverse Gender Gap http://www.nytimes.com/2011/12/14/us/14iht-letter14.html

Trade offs when Mom's the Primary Breadwinner http://blogs.wsj.com/juggle/2009/12/14/trade-offs-when-moms-the-primary-breadwinner/

Women as main wage earners http://www.statcan.gc.ca/studies-etudes/75-001/archive/e-pdf/2457-eng.pdf

Women breadwinners more likely to divorce http://society.ezinemark.com/women-breadwinners-more-likely-to-divorce-study-31887247381.html

Women Breadwinners: When You Make More Money than Him http://eveof87.blogspot.com/2010/09/women-breadwinners-when-you-make-more.html

Women say men's role as breadwinner is no longer relevant http://www.telegraph.co.uk/news/uknews/2039405/Women-say-mens-role-as-breadwinner-is-no-longer-relevant.html

About the author

Jenny Garrett is an executive coach, consultant and speaker. She is passionate about:

* Challenging leaders to make a positive difference
* Motivating women to live their best life
* Inspiring authentic leadership

She is founder of Reflexion Associates, a holistic and expansive leadership development consultancy that has worked internationally over the last ten years to deliver executive coaching and training with a difference: depth, personalisation and meaning.

Jenny's clients are leaders from the corporate world as well as the public and third sector. The common theme is that they want to make positive change, they engage her to help them successfully do just that.

Before becoming an executive coach, Jenny held senior marketing roles in global private sector organisations, where she experienced the complexity of working life. She holds an MA in Management Learning and Leadership as well as a number of coaching qualifications.

You can find her online at www.rockingyourrole.com

Let's connect

As well as the resources referred to in the book:

Guided Visualisation - A podcast which will guide you through creating your vision of the best ME you can be

Drivers - An opportunity to consider your communication approach and what drives your behaviour

Sharing - Guidance on how to start sharing your experience and supporting other MEs

Tummy breathing - Instructions on a breathing exercise to reduce stress and create calm

I will continue to develop new resources, training, leadership programmes, and coaching opportunities to support MEs, so keep in touch via www.rockingyourrole. com for the latest information.

Feel free to share your experience of engaging with the book and let me know how you are Rocking Your Role.

Join the LinkedIn Group: Rocking Your Role

Or tweet me @JenniferGarrett